Including
Gifted, Able
and Talented Children
in the Primary Classroom

Mike Fleetham

Permission to photocopy

This book contains materials which may be reproduced by photocopier or other means for use by the purchaser. The permission is granted on the understanding that these copies will be used within the educational establishment of the purchaser. The book and all its contents remain copyright. Copies may be made without reference to the publisher or the licensing scheme for the making of photocopies operated by the Publishers' Licensing Agency.

Dedication

To four gifted ladies: Doreen, Hannah, Naomi and Emma

Acknowledgements

Thanks to Andrew Pearce for his time, ideas and invaluable contributions to this book – and to all the experts who contributed their stories and experience: Jack, Luke and Dan Priestly; Vicky Swift; Hannah Senior; Emma Clapham; Helen Williams; Leanne Woodley; Traci Forwood; Celia Walker; Debbie McClellan; Mary Phillips.

The right of Mike Fleetham to be identified as the author of this work has been asserted by him in accordance with sections 77 and 78 of the Copyright, Designs and Patents Act 1988.

Including Gifted, Able and Talented Children in the Primary Classroom

MT10786

ISBN-13: 978 1 85503 436 5

© Mike Fleetham

Illustrations © Jorge Santillan

First published 2008

Reprinted 2012, 2014

Printed in the UK for LDA

Pintail Close, Victoria Business Park, Nottingham, NG4 2SG, UK

Contents

1. I need an introduction to this book and to GAT learners

Hi Luke,

I got your e-mail address from your mum – hope you don't mind me getting in touch.

I'm writing a book to help teachers teach Gifted and Talented children more effectively.

I know that you're on the school's G&T register and I wondered if you'd like to share your thoughts and opinions in the book?

This would really help teachers to understand children who've had their talents recognised.

If you're up for this, maybe you could use these questions to guide what you write:

What's school like for you?

What do you do best?

What do you struggle with?

What happens in the lessons you enjoy the most?

What happens in the lessons you enjoy the least?

What advice would you give to a teacher who wants to teach you well?

Thanks Luke,

Mike

Hello Mike,

You wanted to know what school's like for me. Well, I find it gets boring when I've done something before but my strong points are writing action stories and doing shape and times tables up to fifteen. I struggle with extremely descriptive writing and only make silly mistakes. In enjoyable lessons we make shapes and do mini tests. In my least favourite lessons we just copy and are not able to be imaginative.

To be taught well I would need a teacher, in maths, with plenty of back-up work and to make it a task for one year above me. In English I would need a teacher who would let my imagination run wild.

If you need any more information contact me.

Luke

[age 9]

Welcome!

Thanks for reading this book. You'll find it very useful in your work and learning. It's been written to deepen your knowledge of gifted, able and talented (GAT) children and to enrich how you teach them. It takes an inclusive approach: recognising the great proficiency of a small number of children, and also that they are members of full and busy classrooms.

There are many different ways to describe the most successful learners. 'Gifted', 'Talented' and 'Able' appear to be the words used most often. This is shortened to 'GAT' throughout the book.

There are many powerful opinions and questions surrounding GAT. Here are some of the questions:

- Should able children be taught separately or included with everyone else?
- What is a gifted student? A talented learner? An able pupil?
- How should we manage the emotions and esteem of talented individuals?
- Is everyone a GAT learner?
- Are parents partners or problems?

Issues like these are covered practically, without getting hung up on theories and definitions.

Activities are aimed at children up to age 11, though many of the ideas will work just as well in the early secondary-school years. Tasks are designed with GAT learners in mind, but they can easily be used with a mixed-ability group.

To get you to the right information quickly, each section addresses a common need of GAT teachers. With GAT learners in mind, these are:

- identifying learners
- managing provision in your school
- developing yourself and your teaching
- enriching thinking skills
- enriching emotional intelligence
- enriching the curriculum
- involving parents and the wider community.

Theory and practical ideas are included, but the theory is distilled right down and connected to what happens in the classroom. Whether you want to understand before you do, or do and then develop an understanding, this book will meet your needs.

Four steps to defining GAT learners

Let's make sure we know whom we're talking about when we say 'Gifted, able and talented learners'. We'll do this in four simple steps:

- Step 1. Ask an expert (or eight of them).
- Step 2. Address the challenges of defining Gifted, Able and Talented.
- Step 3. Listen to your government.
- Step 4. Customise a definition.

Step 1. Ask an expert (or eight of them)

Every expert in the worlds of GAT education and psychology has something interesting and useful to say about GAT learners. Below is a summary of eight different yet connected views. Together they will help you to develop a deeper understanding of GAT children. The right-hand column describes how each theory makes practical sense when used to define GAT learners.

Expert and what they say ...	*Practically, this means ...*
Joseph Renzulli, Raymond and Lynn Neag Professor of Gifted Education, University of Connecticut Giftedness may be split into two parts: school–house and creative–productive. 1. School–house = success in test-taking and lesson-learning. 2. Creative–productive = success in designing and developing things for a defined audience (e.g. essay, dance, composition, building). Renzulli splits creative–productive into three areas: and argues that a balance between them is needed for giftedness to occur.	The GAT learners will be those who pass your tests, pay attention and do their homework, and those who, when they learn and work: • are motivated to do a task • are more than able to do it • do it with flair and originality • do it for a purpose – e.g. with an audience.
Howard Gardner, John H. and Elisabeth A. Hobbs Professor of Cognition and Education, Harvard Graduate School of Education Intelligence is multi-faceted and everyone has a unique intelligences profile. Each of the following areas of human achievement and potential is equally valuable: • Musical/Rhythmic • Verbal/Linguistic	The GAT learners will be those who excel in making things linked to one or more of the following areas: • making and appreciating music • using language • relating to the natural world • managing relationships with others

Expert and what they say ...	Practically this means ...
• Naturalist • Interpersonal • Intrapersonal • Visual/Spatial • Mathematical/Logical • Bodily/Kinaesthetic. Intelligence is 'the ability to solve problems and create products that are of value to your culture/society'.	• understanding themselves • visual thinking • logical thinking • using body and hands.
David Perkins, formerly Senior Professor of Education, Harvard Graduate School of Education There are three different kinds of intelligence: • neural – the brain's raw processing power • experiential – knowledge acquired by doing • reflective – learning new ways to solve problems and self-monitoring these strategies. Perkins's ideas suggest that: • everyone can become more intelligent • you can teach intelligence to your learners – by providing experiences and problems to solve • intelligence is inclusive. Perkins believes that we can become more intelligent through study and practice, access to appropriate tools and learning to make effective use of those tools.	The GAT learners will be those blessed with quick brains and good memories who can learn by doing and think about their learning. You'll see them learn effectively by studying and by making good use of the resources, materials and experiences that you provide for them.
Carol Dweck, Lewis and Virginia Eaton Professor of Psychology, Stanford University Learners' beliefs about themselves and their abilities contribute to their actual ability level. Entitists believe that personality characteristics and intelligence are fixed. Incrementalists believe that personality and intelligence can grow and change. An entitist self-belief can be limiting; an incrementalist belief can be empowering and motivating. A learner's self-belief is partly constructed by those around them. Dweck argues that 3-year-olds already tend toward entitist or incrementalist, largely due to parental expectations.	The GAT learners may be those who are incrementalists. They believe in themselves and their potential to learn and grow. They'll think and say things such as: • I can. • I can't ... yet. • I can solve this. • There's always a solution. • I can get cleverer. • I'll learn this. • I know how to find it out. • What do I need to know? GAT learners may also be entitist. Although performing well above average, they may have limiting self-belief systems.

Expert and what they say …	Practically this means …
Francoys Gagne, Professor of Psychology, Université du Québec Giftedness is natural human ability (aptitude) in areas such as: • intellectual • creative • social • sensory–motor. Talent is above-average performance in one or more human fields, e.g.: • business • sport • technology • the arts • media. Education helps talent to grow from aptitudes, but personality and social and cultural factors will determine the eventual success of this development.	The GAT learners will be those who are one or more of: • traditionally 'clever' • creative • good with people • kinaesthetically well above average. They will apply these gifts in specific subjects, but their success will depend on: • the learning environment • the opportunities you provide • their personality and motivation. The subjects they do well in may suggest a path to a very successful career.
Abraham Tannenbaum, Professor Emeritus of Education and Psychology, Teachers College, Columbia University Giftedness is the potential to succeed in areas that enrich the moral, physical, emotional, social, intellectual or aesthetic aspects of humanity. Talent is only fully developed in the adult years, but the following are indicators of high potential: • superior general intelligence • exceptional special aptitudes • non-intellectual facilitators (motivation, persistence, curiosity) • environmental influences • chance or luck. Adults show their talents by: • making startling breakthroughs in their field • adding beauty to our environment • succeeding in business and services • using their skills practically.	The GAT learners will be those who show the greatest potential to add value to the lives of others and themselves. You'll look at these children and be thinking things like: • 'Yes, I can just see you as an engineer' • 'She'll be a superb environmentalist when she grows up' • 'He'll make a superb religious leader' • 'I can see him in university doing fantastic research' • 'I just know she'll be a successful artist'. You'll have a good idea who they are because they'll be academically clever and have certain exceptional abilities. They'll also love learning.

Expert and what they say ...	Practically this means ...

Robert Sternberg, American psychologist and psychometrician and Dean of Arts and Sciences at Tufts University
 	
Intelligence may be:
 	
• analytic – ability to reason, solve problems, process information
 	
• creative – ability to combine existing ideas in novel ways
 	
• practical – ability to succeed in real world settings
 	
and any combination of the three, including singly and in pairs. Evidence shows that success is equally likely for any combination.
 	
Sternberg states five necessary criteria for giftedness:
 	
• excellence – superiority to others in some specific area/field
 	
• rarity – high-level skills that few others have
 	
• productivity – using skills and excellence to produce things
 	
• demonstrability – excellence shows in tests and assessments
 	
• value – excellence valued by society.
	The GAT learners will be those who:
	
	• surprise you with their ideas
	  and/or
	
	• have and use great common sense and emotional intelligence in practical situations
	  and/or
	
	• have high academic intelligence.
	
	They'll also be excellent at something that only a very few others are. They'll be able to make things that others value and will do very well in tests.

Lisa Simpson of the animated television series The Simpsons *– she's 8 years old, reads at 14th grade level, and has written a number of high-quality essays* Giftedness relates to a wide range of natural abilities and is largely independent of environment. Simpson argues that giftedness and talent are both manifestations of these abilities and are exhibited in one or more of the following ways: • musical ability • interpersonal skills • coping strategies (tolerance, patience, understanding, assertiveness, perseverance, charm, 'likeability') • moral and ethical integrity • intellectual competence • cognitive processing skills (reasoning, problem-solving) • cognitive function (memory, speed of thinking). Counter-intuitively, Simpson further states that the development of high ability in these areas may be aided by a family setting which does not recognise, value and celebrate such gifts.	The GAT learners will be those who survive and succeed in spite of their circumstances. They will most likely lack one or more of the following: • parental support • life opportunities • financial affluence • love • friends • learning resources. These are the quick-witted, lovable, bright shining stars who you want to take home with you and give a large tasty meal and a warm bed.

Step 2. Address the challenges of defining Gifted, Able and Talented

Challenge 1 – expert views

Individually, each expert mentioned says something valuable about GAT learners, and together they bring us a little closer to a workable definition. Let's look at the common themes in their thinking:

- Gifts, abilities and talents are related yet different.
- GAT learners are intelligent (intelligence may be defined in many ways).
- Giftedness, ability and talent cover a wide range of human endeavour.
- 'GATness' is dependent on the environment/culture/society in which it's measured.
- GAT learners produce things of very high quality.
- There are many ways to define GATness.

Challenge 2 – many definitions

Individuals, schools, local authorities and governments define GATness in many different ways.

No one definition is perfect – highly able children can no more be fitted into one neat category box than any other child (Council for the Curriculum Examination and Assessment, Ireland 2006).

In 1996, D. McAlpine came up with a way to categorise definitions ('Who are the Gifted and Talented?' In D. McAlpine and R. Moltzen (eds.), *Gifted and Talented: New Zealand Perspectives*, Palmerston North: ERDC Press, Massey University). He suggested that we may place a definition along three scales:

1. From conservative to liberal: how many areas of gift and talent are included in the definition and how many people will feature

---
Conservative   Liberal

2. From single to multi-dimensional: how many different abilities are included in a definition

---
Single   Multi-dimensional

3. From performance to potential: whether a person is already achieving highly or has the possibility of achieving highly in an area

---
Performance   Potential

Challenge 3 – language

Gift? Talent? Ability? Skill? Aptitude? Intelligence? Excellence?

Giftedness suggests an excellence bestowed for free. It may take on religious or spiritual overtones. *Talent* has to be worked at, but from an advantageous starting point. *Ability* seems neutral, while *aptitude* implies potential to achieve. *Intelligence* is Pandora's box and *excellence* is laden with value judgement.

We could wrestle over what each of these means until the cows come home, but it's more practical to define the characteristics of our most successful learners first and then give them a name. 'GAT learner' is used in this book.

Step 3. Listen to your government

Large-scale national provision for GAT learners needs nationally agreed definitions. Here are examples.

Gifted and talented children are those who have one or more abilities developed to a level significantly ahead of their year group (or with the potential to develop these abilities).

Talented: Top 5–10% of pupils per school as measured by actual or potential achievement in the subjects of Art, Music, PE, Games

Gifted: Top 5–10% of pupils per school as measured by actual or potential achievement in the other curriculum subjects.

DfES 2005, 2007

Pupils who require extended opportunities across the curriculum in order to develop their abilities in one or more areas.

Welsh Parliament 2003

Many countries in the world call these young people gifted and talented and certainly our Scottish pupils have exceptional abilities in a whole range of areas, however in keeping with our inclusive approach to education in Scotland we prefer to call our pupils 'more able'. In many ways, what we call them doesn't matter, what is important is that their abilities are recognised, challenged and celebrated.

Scottish Network for Able Pupils

To extend this a little, the definition of gifted and talented in one school in India is directly related to its country's social and developmental needs:

The purpose of the school is to educate gifted and talented students not only for academics, but for motivation to help their state, country, and the world. The school is indigenous, based on the philosophy of Swami Vivekananda. The rhetoric of the field of the education of the gifted and talented is that bright students are our future leaders. This school in India seems more geared to producing leaders than does current gifted education in the United States.

Jane Piirto, *Gifted Child Quarterly*, Vol. 46, No. 3, 181–192 (2002)

Step 4. Customise a definition

Everyone reading this book will have a slightly different take on GAT learners. Treat the following definition like clay: mould it into a shape that's right for you, your colleagues and your pupils:

GAT learners are those who do, or could do, something of value much better than others.

To customise this, you'll need to decide three things:

1. What 'something of value' is and who's doing the valuing.
2. What 'much better' means in your organisation.
3. Who the 'others' are.

In this book, 'something of value' includes not only subject-based achievement but personal skills and characteristics too. The words 'or could do' suggest potential and the educator's duty to dig deep into each learner to find the gifts, talents and abilities hidden therein. And 'much better' and 'others' should be specific to your situation – classroom, school or authority – but should be chosen so that the GAT learners are significant and noticeable.

Here are three sample definitions, each created from the same generic starting point. Each one would identify different children as GAT and each one suits a different school ethos.

Gifted, able and talented learners are those whose (potential) achievement in one or more of the multiple intelligences is equivalent to the expected standard of children who are three or more years older.

Gifted, able and talented learners are those who achieve at least 125 in our standardised tests.

Gifted, able and talented learners are those who demonstrate one or more of the following skills significantly better than others in their year group: leadership, creative thinking, problem-solving, learning skills, relationship management, self-management.

To finish this section, read what happens when a talent is removed from its usual, defining context:

Aboriginals were able to navigate great distances by using 'songlines'. They would 'sing' the route they needed to take. These were not just a series of directions but a song-cycle which also incorporated Dreamtime creation myths describing the features/landmarks they would need to follow. Author Bruce Chatwin travelled to Australia to investigate this cultural phenomenon. At one point in his journey he describes how his aboriginal guide was muttering to himself at incredible speed. The reason for the rapid muttering? The 'song' was meant to be recited at the rhythm and pace of a walking man, not – as in this case – that of a four-wheel drive Landcruiser.

2. I need ideas for identifying my GAT learners

Once you've settled on your definition of GAT learners, you'll need quick and effective ways to find them. Your identification methods will need to relate to your definition. For example, a liberal, multi-dimensional and potential-orientated definition requires liberal, multi-dimensional and potential-orientated identification methods. So, if you're looking for a wide range of skills and abilities, then you should cast many different nets widely. Likewise, if you've chosen a conservative, restricted, performance-orientated definition, use a fishing rod and one type of bait.

Build a straightforward system that works for your GAT learners and your fellow teachers. Once you've set it up and tried it out, change it in the light of experience. If one identification method adds nothing to the search, drop it. If another one homes in on GATs like spotlights on a stage, keep it.

Here I present eight different approaches to use. They can be used individually or in combination. The first four are remote (without the learner present). The other four rely on interaction with (or observation of) the learner. You are recommended to use at least one from each group.

Remote
- Performance data
- Work samples
- Checklists
- Personalised learning profiles

Interactive
- Questions and answers
- Parents
- Anecdotes and observed spontaneous acts
- Self/Peer reflection

Performance data

Schools usually have lots of data readily to hand: National Curriculum test results (SATs), standardised tests (verbal/non-verbal), cognitive abilities test (CATs), various diagnostic tests (reading, spelling, etc.); informal class tests (spellings, multiplication tables). The results are applied in many ways:

- to rank/order children in their class/year group;
- to compare schools in league tables;
- to produce benchmarking data so a school is compared to others in similar socio-economic areas;
- to plan for future educational provision;
- to allocate resources;
- to inform future lessons / curriculum organisation.

It can also help you find your GAT learners.

A child performing consistently well in a variety of tests measuring different abilities, or exceptionally well in tests focused on one area, could be identified as GAT – or perhaps their gift is test-taking! Watch out, though. I wouldn't measure the passage of time with kitchen scales, so make sure you understand the limitations of the measuring instruments in your hands and exactly what they are measuring.

Most national and commercial standardised tests come with instructions and guidance on the interpretation of results. GAT learners will be those who score higher than a certain number. For example, 130+ on the NFER standardised reading test puts the child in the top 1 per cent. However, a child who scores 100 per cent accuracy on a single word-reading test may be reading text at the literal level and have poor comprehension skills. Those children who have a well-developed memory (a talent in its own right) may score highly on tests that require factual recall. That does not necessarily mean that they are able to apply their vast knowledge in a purposeful or creative way.

▶ GAT-spotting suggestion No. 1

A single test score only records performance from a single moment in time. Look for a history of consistently high scores in different types of tests.

Work samples

Like test scores, children's work samples provide a snapshot of what they achieved at a certain time on a certain day. A single exemplary piece may suggest GATness, but doesn't confirm it. Further evidence – both broad and deep – is usually needed. 'Broad' here means different types of evidence from different sources, and 'deep' means evidence collected over time. When hunting for excellence in the marking pile, be mindful of a couple of things:

1. *Each piece of work is standing alone.* Its author/creator is not present to explain, justify, describe and answer questions. If they were, how would a discussion alter your understanding of their product?

2. *The method of presentation may hide the ability.* Can musical genius show itself through writing?

If writing is being used to assess anything other than written language, the quality of the writing must be completely detached from the ability being assessed. And if a true picture cannot be established with pen and paper, then alternative evidence is needed.

If you have chosen a multi-dimensional definition of GAT, then your identification methods should be multi-dimensional too – not only written. Here are a few examples.

I'm looking for	Work sample could be
Mathematical gifts, talents and ability	Mental maths test, written solutions to problems
Social gifts, talents and ability	Video evidence of social interactions
Leadership gifts, talents and ability	Recorded testimonies of children who've worked in the same group (who have 'been led')

▶ GAT-spotting suggestion No. 2

For each potential GAT learner examine three different work samples collected over time.

Checklists

Checklists, like data and work samples, imply GATness rather than confirm it. A GAT checklist describes common features of a typical GAT learner, and therein lie two interesting points:

1. The assumption that all GAT learners share common features.
2. The risk of stereotyping learners and labelling them with specific characteristics.

GAT checklists usually suggest implicitly that a typical GAT learner is a frustrated specialist, or all-rounder who has difficulty expressing themselves. Here are things that often appear on a checklist:

- ❑ **is a good all-rounder**
- ❑ **is a high achiever in one area**
- ❑ **has poor writing skills**
- ❑ **has a short attention span**
- ❑ **has behavioural problems**

- ❑ **tries hard to disguise their abilities**
- ❑ **has the potential to achieve more**
- ❑ **is creative and thinks creatively**
- ❑ **asks challenging questions**
- ❑ **prefers to be with adults / older children.**

There is nothing wrong with a checklist that includes these items. In fact, it'll pick up more than just the GAT learners for you – those with poor social skills, for example. Use it if you wish, but I do recommend creating your own. This is because you'll have a unique definition of GATness and the checklist should be tied to that, rather than to someone else's definition.

◉ GAT-spotting suggestion No. 3

Create your own GAT checklist:

1. **Create the items on your checklist directly from your own definition of GAT learners.**
2. **Include references to learning *and* behaviour.**
3. **Keep it simple – 10 tick boxes are faster than 30 items graded from 1 to 4.**
4. **Decide how to interpret the results – Are certain ticks essential? How many ticks = GATness?**

Personalised learning profiles

A personalised learning profile (PLP) reveals a student's learning preferences and therefore describes how to make learning more effective and enjoyable for them. There are many ways to describe these preferences, such as: learning styles, multiple intelligences, thinking styles and personality types. Each GAT learner (like everyone else) has their own unique way of learning and many distinctive learning traits.

As with checklists, we should try to avoid assumptions and stereotyping. However, GAT learners may well have some qualities in common. Using her on-line learning styles analysis, Barbara Prashnig has identified the traits of what she terms 'gifted learners'. These are students who learn well, regardless of subject area. Their talent is simply learning. Prashnig's learning style model includes six layers:

- neurological preferences
- sensory preferences
- physical needs

- environmental factors
- social influences
- learner attitudes/dispositions.

It indicates the where, when, how and with whom of taking in new or difficult information. Prashnig asserts that 'gifted learners' generally have the following characteristics:

- Neurological preferences – integrated between analytic and holistic thinking (logical and intuitive).
- Sensory preferences – multi-sensory: can learn equally well by seeing, hearing, doing and touching.
- Physical needs – have no particular preference for time of day, movement or intake (of snacks).
- Environmental factors – tend to avoid noise/music and informal work areas.
- Social influences – prefer to work alone or with like-minded friends and avoid authority.
- Learner attitudes/dispositions – highly motivated, extremely persistent and non-conforming.

If you could observe these preferences easily, then you'd have an interesting GAT checklist. However, displaying these features does not guarantee GATness and lacking them does not preclude it. Both of the following students achieved over 95 per cent in their test:

Emily is studying for a French test. She is lying on the bed amidst a sprawl of books, radio playing in the background, nibbling at a cream cracker.

Lee sits studying at a tidy desk in a well-lit room. It's quiet and 10.15 in the morning. At the top of the desk is a revision timetable.

As teachers, our own PLP may heavily influence us. The question we need to ask is: 'How does my classroom and my teaching style allow GAT learners to show their strengths and to thrive?'

Can't you see I'm working?

○ GAT-spotting suggestion No. 4

Use your definition of GAT to audit your classroom environment and teaching style. For example, if your definition includes 'leadership', 'creativity' and 'high-order thinking', look for resources and lessons that allow these abilities to be used and developed. GAT learners with these skills will rise to the challenge and identify themselves to you through their success.

Questions and answers

Talking with children provides you with an ongoing assessment of their abilities and potential. Asking learners different types of question is a major part of this, as is allowing them to ask their own.

Just as in tests, we can ask questions that require factual recall – for example, 'What is the capital of Liechtenstein? How do you spell Liechtenstein? Who went to Liechtenstein for their holiday?' These are closed questions – they have only one possible answer. Some closed questions have multiple specific answers – for example 'What are the days of the week?'

An open question – for example 'What would you like to find out about the country of Liechtenstein?' – may have many individual responses, as may more creative stimuli such as 'If Leichtenstein were a piece of furniture [or a building / musical instrument / animal], what would it be?'

GAT learners may well be those who give off-the-wall answers in class, and those who have equally bizarre questions for you. They may also make persistent, obsessive enquiry into a specific topic.

◉ GAT-spotting suggestion No. 5

Ask a variety of questions regularly in class. As well as: 'What, When, Where and Who', use 'How, Why and What if'. Children who are GAT for memory skills respond to the first set; those who excel in reasoning, problem-solving and creativity rise to the second.

◉ GAT-spotting suggestion No. 6

Value and record children's bizarre and out-of-context questions. 'How fast does rain go?' in the middle of literacy, or 'Why do leaves crackle in autumn?' during maths. Similar, peculiar questions (and answers) may indicate GAT thinking, and their subject matter may point to an area of actual or potential specialism.

Parents

Chapter 7 provides suggestions for building effective relationships with the parents of GAT learners. When it comes to identifying GATness, parents/carers are an invaluable resource. Whether they realise it or not, they are experts on the subject of their own children and should be respected as such.

The question 'Are we talking about the same child?' is one that has been frequently asked (or thought) at parent–teacher meetings. Delighted, but slightly bemused, parents are informed about their child's conscientious, co-operative behaviour and progress in creative writing, whilst trying to relate this to the demanding, argumentative telly addict with whom they are familiar. Then there are the difficult meetings, where the teacher, diplomatically, describes a child with challenging behaviour, poor concentration and general underachievement to parents who experience a happy-go-lucky individual who is polite, helpful and always making things. Both scenarios may describe a GAT learner.

Effective communication with parents may draw the big picture of a child. If you are a parent as well as a teacher, consider what you would most want your own child's teacher to know. Then give opportunities to your pupils' parents to share equivalent information with you. Also ask yourself what you need to know from these parents in your quest to find the GAT learners.

Early on in year 3, Emily suffered from flu. In the months that followed, she would become exhausted after physical exertion such as swimming, bike-riding or even a long walk. She would be unable to concentrate, become ill-tempered and need to sleep. By making Emily's teachers aware of this condition her parents avoided a situation in which a normally gifted, conscientious and co-operative child might have been seen as someone developing a behaviour problem.

◉ GAT-spotting suggestion No. 7

During your first formal meeting with parents/carers, find out what (if any) gifts, talents and abilities they believe their child possesses.

Anecdotes and observed spontaneous acts

Up to now, the GAT identification methods have been planned events. This one isn't.

Why was Sherlock Holmes so successful? He had fantastic general knowledge, but so do lots of other people – especially if they are fictional. Sir Arthur Conan Doyle bestowed on his flawed hero the gift of observation. Holmes noticed small details and interpreted their significance using his knowledge.

Our own senses are bombarded with so much information that we sometimes miss the details and overlook the connections. Becoming aware of significant details and important connections is the kind of skill we need to develop in order to identify GAT learners.

Apparently, walls have ears. If only they could talk. Staffrooms reverberate with anecdotes. What may seem a trivial throw-away story may be a valuable insight into a child. Their quirky answers may indicate highly original thinking. Their misbehaviour may point to unrecognised talents. And the pickles into which they get themselves may highlight a mismatch between learning style and teaching style. Next time someone is telling you an anecdote, take a little time to reflect and ask 'Is this a GAT learner?'

Apply your newly developed skills to first-hand observations. As the words suggest, spontaneous acts may happen any time, anywhere. Create the right conditions for them to occur – by offering tasks that have more than one possible outcome, problems with a variety of solutions, opportunities to work with different learners and chances to create.

Is a child deviating from a prescribed method because they are having difficulty sequencing a process, or are they thinking outside the box? Dean (year 5) could subtract large numbers (ThHTU) using his own method, he could explain the method; and he could perform the calculations faster than his teacher. Dean was encouraged by his teacher to continue with his own methods and achieved a level 5 in year 6.

⦿ GAT-spotting suggestion No. 8

Set up a Sherlock folder: one blank page for each learner in a ring binder. When a spontaneous, GATworthy event takes place, you can scribble it on a Post-it® note and then fix it to the relevant child's page.

Self/Peer reflection

What do you think you are good at? What do you enjoy doing the most? Why? This should probably be the first stop when trying to identify GAT learners. In a supportive environment learners are often eager to tell you their strengths and favourite activities. However, there are plenty of reasons why learners will not tell you: peer pressure to dumb down, low self-esteem, poor self-perception or just plain modesty. Depending upon circumstances, reassurance may have to be given that information divulged in questionnaires or discussed in interviews will remain confidential.

Peers are often happy to elaborate on each other's achievements both in positive ways (Can Sarah be on our team? She's brilliant.) and negative ways (Arvo's a swot!). They are often able to provide information about activities outside school life. It's grist to the mill of identifying GAT learners.

○ GAT-spotting suggestion No. 9

Send learners off with cardboard magnifying glasses to find the talents in the room/school. Provide prompts: 'What are you best at?', 'What are you good at outside school?'

A sample GAT identification system

Make your GAT identification system manageable, flexible and effective. All evidence must be considered against your definition of GAT. Here's a sample four-stage process:

1. Indication (before the school year begins)
   - Look at the evidence (test scores, anecdotes, work samples, PLPs, already on GAT register).
   - Select those children who are likely to be GAT learners.

2. Investigation (during first half-term)
   - Talk to the parents of children who may be GAT.
   - Ask class teachers to nominate GAT learners.
   - Collect further work samples.
   - Complete GAT checklists.

3. Confirmation (by the end of the first term and ongoing)
   - Gather spontaneous evidence and further work samples.
   - Add new GAT learners to register.

4. Evaluation (in the last half-term)
   - Review the identification process and adapt as required.
   - Review GAT register – should anyone be removed/added?

The following research indicates the type of identification that we teachers prefer:

A US study examined a national sample of classroom teachers, teachers of the gifted, administrators, and consultants from rural, suburban, and urban areas regarding their assumptions about the gifted identification process. Respondents indicated the degree to which they agreed or disagreed with 20 items that reflected guidelines for a comprehensive (GAT) identification system. Five factors were derived from 20 items. Respondents favored the use of individual expression criteria, ongoing assessment, multiple criteria for identification, and consideration of contextual factors. Teachers of the gifted and respondents from urban areas were more likely to favor these strategies. The sample opposed restricting identification to the sole use of achievement or IQ scores.

Renzulli et al., *Gifted Child Quarterly*, Vol. 49, No. 1, 68–79 (2005)

The definition and the identification of GAT learners are related like a building to its foundations. The definition forms the cornerstones upon which the walls of identification are built.

Now you know who your GAT learners are, how do you provide for them in school? Read on.

3. I need ideas for managing GAT provision in my school

Mary's story

Mary excelled academically at junior school, particularly in music. However, the school favoured sport, which was not Mary's forte, and, as a result, she lost confidence in her accomplishments, feeling that her successes were valued less than those of her more sporting classmates.

Mary's experience of secondary school was better, although she decided it would be safer to keep quiet about her gifts. She would have benefited from the opportunity to wrestle with concepts and ideas, but this was not encouraged. If Mary completed her tasks ahead of others, her teachers rarely gave her more work to do. Mary would have risen to the challenge of complex extension work.

Mary recalls that throughout her school career no prizes were awarded for academic achievements, except for an ad hoc presentation for O-level grades, which the school never repeated.

After secondary school, Mary went on to study medicine at Cambridge University and psychiatry at the Maudsley Hospital, London. She is currently one of the youngest professors in the UK, leading teams in London and Pittsburg, and carrying out innovative neuroscientific research.

Despite a far from perfect school experience, Mary remembers many teachers who contributed to her success: 'They all had an ability to identify and encourage individual talent.'

If you are responsible for the GAT provision in your school, I hope this chapter will make your position of leadership and responsibility easier. I asked friends and colleagues already doing the job to share their insights, their thinking and their tips. I have added their words at the end of the chapter.

Three Ps

The DCSF website http://ygt.dcsf.gov.uk includes a matrix of quality standards in GAT education and offers a framework for best practice and guidance for developing provision. The role of managing GAT provision is in three parts: policy, people and practice.

Policy:

- evolving an approach, ethos and policy
- maintaining a GAT register
- recording and reporting on GAT provision.

People:

- supporting and coaching teachers
- developing support staff
- liaising with parents and the community
- supporting learners' transitions
- establishing links with other schools and organisations.

Practice:

- fulfilling statutory requirements for teaching and learning
- identifying GAT learners
- keeping up to date with and sharing the best GAT practice
- identifying and providing suitable resources and experiences
- leading by example and enriching school practice
- monitoring and evaluating teaching and learning.

The list is illustrative, not exhaustive.

Policy

The policy aspects of your role cover the formalities and the administration. Written requirements, records and reports are not everyone's favourites, but they are essential for monitoring, accountability and the development of provision. Paperwork should be minimal (maximise the time spent doing the job, not writing about it). Try the following paper-check procedure. Before you generate a new piece of paper or paper-based system, ask the following questions:

1. Is it a legal requirement that I produce it?
2. Is there an alternative method?
3. Can an existing system be adapted instead?
4. How will it add value to my GAT learners and GAT teachers?

I recommend that you have three short documents: a GAT policy, audit and register.

GAT policy

A policy is essential. It expresses an agreed philosophy and a shared approach. It should be flicked through, not filed, and should answer the following questions:

1. Why has this policy been written?
2. What do we aspire to achieve through this policy?
3. How do we describe, identify and monitor our GAT learners?
4. How do we teach for our GAT learners?
5. How do we organise our GAT teaching?
6. What is the role of the GAT co-ordinator?
7. What resources do we provide for our GAT learners?
8. How do we communicate with other schools on behalf of our GAT learners?
9. How do we link with local, national and international organisations to benefit our GAT learners?
10. How do we inform, involve and interact with parents of GAT learners?
11. When and how do we review this policy?

There's no reason for the policy to stretch much past a single side of A4 paper. When you write the policy, consult all stakeholders – learners, teachers, parents and governors. You could gather ideas during a staff meeting, a parents' meeting or a school council meeting.

Teacher carousel

1. Write the following key questions on flipchart paper, put one on each of five tables, then organise one small group at each table.

Who are the GAT learners?	How do we teach for GAT learners?	Why do we need a GAT policy?	What resources do GAT learners need?	How do we liaise with parents and organisations?

2. Small groups spend a minute or so discussing their question and writing their responses on the paper.
3. All groups then move on to the next question, read the existing answers, and add their own.
4. When all groups have visited all questions and returned to their starting point, decide which three answers are most important for each question.
5. Base your draft policy on these answers.

Audit

An audit breathes life into the policy. It helps you to describe where you are, celebrate what you've achieved and plan for improvements. See the example. Your audit needs to include something like it for each part of your policy. Use highlighter pens to indicate where you're at.

	Not there yet	*Done it!*	*Where next?*
Describe	No shared agreement on which learners are GAT	Shared agreement exists on what a GAT learner is	Procedure in place for annual review of GAT description
Identify	No procedure in place for identifying GAT learners	Procedure in place for identifying GAT learners	Procedure in place for annual review of GAT identification
Monitor	No procedure in place for monitoring GAT provision	Procedure in place for monitoring GAT provision	Procedure in place for annual review of GAT monitoring

Register

A register is needed to keep track of every GAT learner. I recommend it includes:

- name, class, date of birth, ethnic group, gender
- identified gift, ability or talent
- when identified and by whom
- QCA scores and NC levels
- other assessment details (IQ/CAT/dyslexia, etc.)
- learning style and multiple intelligences profiles
- description of current in-school and out-of-school provision
- notes on meetings with parents and external agencies
- monitoring and review arrangements
- additional notes.

People

Strong and effective relationships are the foundation of any leadership role. The people you'll need to build them with are:

- school managers
- teachers
- support staff
- learners
- parents
- members of the community
- other organisations.

We've already thought about parents (page 17), so let's consider the remaining people in the list.

School managers: You may be a school manager in addition to having GAT responsibility. If not, the key to success is communication. Make sure that the school leadership team knows how you are fulfilling your GAT role. Establish what they expect of you. The ongoing conversation should define the levels of support you can expect and the tasks to be carried out. Ask, suggest, advise, inform, seek advice and share successes and challenges.

Teachers: Some colleagues may be wary, expecting paperwork, resources and requests for time to come flying their way. Others may feel challenged in teaching GAT learners – some of whom may have abilities more advanced than their own. It's important therefore to cast yourself in the role of servant rather than guru and make it clear that part of your job is to support them.

Support staff: Over recent years the role of support staff has changed out of all recognition. Well-meaning parents who signed up to assist now find themselves taking whole classes to cover planning, preparation and assessment time. Some relish the opportunity, others stick to the sticking. Bear this in mind as you involve your support staff in the GAT provision. They hold invaluable facts that the class teacher often doesn't get to hear. Classroom assistants are able to form different relationships because of the way they work.

Make use of this knowledge. An assistant may have evidence of an ability that has gone unnoticed through formal assessment. Or they may have the time and resources to provide emotional and intellectual support to GAT learners. Support staff will also bring their own gifts into school. Find out what these are. You may be able to build them into the curriculum.

Learners: The relationship that a teacher has with their pupils is one of the cornerstones of learning success. GAT learners need to know that you value them and that their differences are seen as strengths, not disabilities. Relationships take time to build and need commitment and understanding from both sides. This may be especially important if the learner clearly has abilities that outshine the teacher's. Watch out for the Hermione–Snape effect: Severus Snape, teacher in the Harry Potter series of books and films, maintains a poisonous dislike for GAT learner Hermione Granger. She is clearly the most able student in the year, yet he consistently ignores her and puts her down. He is threatened and intimidated by her stunning abilities. Thankfully, Hermione retains the emotional resilience to weather his regular and predictable attacks. See page 48 (Emma's story) for a real-life example of the Hermione–Snape effect.

Practice

When it comes to pedagogy, some of your colleagues may see you as the fount of all GAT wisdom and a source of sound practical advice.

Others may reckon they could do the job better than you. Some may be only interested in using your GAT budget for their own subjects, while occasionally someone will give you positive and realistic feedback on how well you're doing, and thank you for setting a fine example with GAT learners.

Be aware of what colleagues think of you and your role, but try not to define yourself by their opinions. The bottom line is that you are responsible for GAT provision and you are there to serve the GAT learners' best interests.

One of the best ways to model good practice is to present yourself as a learner – both of the GAT role and as a classroom practitioner. You don't expect to be an expert overnight, but be willing and able to learn from experience and build up your knowledge. This approach may help you avoid unfair criticism when you are asked to model good practice for colleagues. It also sets a fine example to all learners. It's OK to say 'I don't know yet – I'll find out' or 'That could have gone better. Next time I think I'll …' or 'That was great – I'll do more of it.'

There are three main ways to help your teachers to develop their practice for GAT learners.

Enrichment: Learning experiences take study of a subject into different areas – beyond the limits usually set by the curriculum.

For example, a gifted geographer could be given opportunities to:

- visit and study a variety of places – urban, suburban and country
- work with practising geographers, geologists and earth scientists
- study favourite places and peoples, with appropriate time and resources
- prepare and carry out surveys on human behaviour.

Extension: Learning experiences are given that develop a particular area in terms of higher-order thinking. They also aim to help students work and learn independently.

A gifted geographer could be given opportunities to:

- analyse the environmental impact of a new recyling centre on local services
- create an imaginative solution to urban overcrowding
- evaluate the effectiveness of two different subway systems.

Acceleration: Learning experiences with older learners and/or involving work designed for older learners are given. Tests and exams may also be taken earlier than expected.

A gifted geographer could sit GCSE Geography in year 9.

Many practical suggestions and resources to improve teaching for GAT learners appear in Chapter 6.

GAT professional profiles

Every professional who works with and for GAT learners will have their own approach. You will develop your role and responsibility in a different way from the next GAT co-ordinator. But it can be helpful to look at where others have already walked – there is no sense in reinventing the GAT wheel. Here are the profiles of five successful professionals which may help you to design or clarify your own role. You may like to answer for yourself the prompts that I gave them:

- I believe that … (personal philosophy about GAT teaching and learning)
- My work involves … (leadership role)
- The biggest challenges are …
- My greatest successes/achievements are …

Debbie McClellan, G&T Strand Co-ordinator / Teaching and Learning Strand Manager, South East Northumberland Excellence Partnership, England

Personal philosophy about GAT teaching and learning:

- It is not élitist. GAT teaching and learning is 'good-quality' teaching and learning; a rich, varied, creative diet of classroom provision allows any number of gifts and talents to emerge.
- Good-quality teaching may take a little more thought but ultimately it involves a lot less effort. Increasing pupil thinking and talking time, offering more choice, allowing greater freedom, being less didactic: all of this means they are doing more of the work! Hand over as much responsibility as they can manage effectively and everybody wins!
- All children are vastly more capable than they are generally given credit for. When presented with the opportunity, most of them amaze us with their thinking and creativity.
- A greater explicit emphasis on skills rather than content may not be flavour of the month with middle England, but who would you rather have working with you: someone with finite factual knowledge or someone with an infinite capacity to find things out?
- We should ask if we need to find out what our schools are doing wrong – or if our energy would be better spent in finding out what they're doing right and encouraging them to do more of it. There is a huge amount of excellent practice – it must be made more widespread and consistent.
- 'GAT' doesn't need to be yet another stick-shaped initiative with which to beat teachers. Shame about the label because 'GAT' is so much more; it is creativity, confidence, challenge, aspiration, personalisation, responsibility, independence, curiosity, problem-solving, self-awareness, resilience, risk-taking, accountability, ownership, excellence, enjoyment, enthusiasm, endurance, questioning, pride, competition, negotiation, diligence – and that might just be the teacher's!

My work involves …

- Identifying, sharing and celebrating good practice
- Working alongside colleagues to develop successful strategies and trial innovative practice
- Encouraging partnership working between schools
- Offering advice and suggestions – and finding out answers when I don't know them

- Being a sounding board
- Trying, possibly failing but learning together (being prepared to take risks)
- Remaining positive and upbeat.

The biggest challenges for me in this role are ...

- Reminding teachers what great skills they already have
- Overcoming the 'not another initiative!' hurdle
- Convincing teachers they can be creative and pupil centred and still achieve objectives
- Having so much to learn in such a short time.

My greatest successes/achievements are ...

- Building up really positive relationships in all of our schools – being credible is vital
- Showing that pupils can have choice about how and what they learn without the loss of control
- Offering innovative and worthwhile training opportunities
- Leading a working party to create a useful resource bank for first schools
- Learning *so much* from others and being able to share that knowledge between the schools.

Celia Walker, Gifted and Talented Co-ordinator, Solent Junior School, Hampshire

I believe that GAT teaching and learning should be ...

- for all pupils as everyone can benefit at their own level
- an integral part of the curriculum, not an add-on for a few
- exciting, creative and not within the confines of a typical didactic approach
- constantly evolving.

My school role involves ...

- managing the GAT register (been going for about ten years)
- analysing pupils' learning styles and providing advice/guidance to them, the parents and the teacher
- arranging workshops/visits/activities, etc. to enhance the curriculum provision for all pupils
- providing suitable resources / guidance for staff / updates about GAT provision
- introducing new initiatives
- monitoring planning, delivery (for higher-order thinking skills, learning styles, extension and enrichment activities) and pupil achievement
- networking with other subject managers in the school and other GAT managers.

The biggest challenges are ...

- keeping all the staff on board, interested and fresh in their approach
- making sure that parents really understand about the needs of their children (that provision is about offering a breadth of experiences in other fields) and their role in the process
- tackling underachievement, especially in boys
- getting everything done in the time available.

My greatest successes/achievements are …

- persuading all staff to consider different learning styles and plan/deliver accordingly
- the introduction of higher-order thinking skills so that they are now an integral part of lessons
- being instrumental in the creation of a positive teaching and learning environment in which all children feel valued, successful and proud of their achievements
- keeping my personal interest and development fresh and keen for the last ten years.

Traci Forwood, Gifted and Talented Resource Teacher, Carroll County, Maryland, USA

Personal philosophy about G and T teaching and learning:

- Children who feel respected and are motivated/inspired achieve great things.
- It is important to look at each individual child's needs and not label them.
- Children need to be challenged and learn to see setbacks as opportunities for growth and progress.
- GT students often possess unique characteristics and behaviors which require differentiated instruction and support (social and emotional needs are often different from their peers).
- Students need to learn their strengths and weaknesses and use this to their advantage.
- Students need ample time for discussion and exploration.
- A good teacher asks good questions.

My work involves …

- Identifying students who need GT services.
- Direct instruction of 3rd to 5th grade GT students in math and language arts once per week.
- Visiting primary classrooms and exposing them to various thinking strategies, during which the classroom teacher observes the students, noting those who seem to 'bubble up'.
- Research and staff development.
- Parental support and education.
- Curriculum development based on research and National Association for Gifted Children standards.

The biggest challenges for me in this role are …

- Fitting the above responsibilities in (most schools only have a part-time GT teacher in my county).
- Working with a diverse group of teachers, some of whom are not receptive to ideas or support.
- Some teachers who do not understand GT students' unique needs, feel threatened by highly intelligent children, and perceive their questioning and behaviors as disrespectful.
- Finding a way to ensure that students who have other passions and gifts are recognized – not just those who perform well on written assignments and those who are attentive and compliant.
- Lack of arts in the GT program.
- Creating a relationship and 'synergy' with a student, only to have them return to an environment or home where there is no support.

My greatest successes/achievements are …

- Inspiring and encouraging students to do more than they thought they could.
- Helping children with ADHD or another 'learning disability' to see their unique talents/gifts.
- Collaborating with others in my field and seeking out research to refine continually our delivery of instruction to meet the needs of our students best.
- Continue each day as a lifelong learner with the faith that I will make a difference in someone's life today, no matter how small it may be.
- Earning the trust of parents, students and colleagues.

The GT Education Program of Carroll County's mission statement (from www.carrollk12.org/instruction/GT/index.htm, with minor amendments) is:

Carroll County Public Schools' Gifted and Talented Education Program, as an integral part of the community learning culture, will provide identified students with a continuum of services based on sound theory and research to meet the needs of highly able learners and maximize student achievement.

Leanne Woodley, Learning Officer, Special Education K-12, Wollongong, New South Wales, Australia

Personal philosophy about GAT teaching and learning:

- All teachers have a responsibility to educate all students to their full academic, emotional, social, sporting and spiritual potential. Opportunities for students to achieve their full potential in all these areas should be embedded in quality and diverse learning experiences.
- Schools need to provide optimum opportunities for all students to engage as active, creative and critical thinkers while extending and deepening their understanding.

My work involves supporting …

- Schools with the identification of gifted students.
- Teachers with classroom strategies to differentiate the curriculum for students.
- Teachers to find engaging ways to extend students' knowledge and skills and explore values.

The biggest challenge for me in this role is helping teachers understand the difference between gifted and talented.

- Building awareness in teachers that it is OK to go beyond the norm – to think outside the square of the standard curriculum to engage and extend learners.
- Supporting teachers to think beyond the stereotypical ideas of who might be gifted. Teachers need to be encouraged to identify students who may be gifted but have a specific learning difficulty or the gifted underachievers and gifted children from other cultures.

My greatest successes/achievements are …

- Running a professional development course titled 'Diversifying Learning Experiences.' The course explores learning and teaching in the mixed-ability classroom; gifted education; identifying student needs; students with a learning difficulty; emotional learning strategies; different cognitive taxonomies/strategies to engage learners – e.g. Bloom's, MI, Thinker Keys, Question Matrix, critical thinking/questions; documentation – policy and guidelines; assessment for and of learning.

Anything else you'd like to add …

- Over the past year our team has been encouraging schools to design a plan for G&T in their schools which includes actively engaging parents and carers, building awareness of resources available, respecting differences, identification procedures, flexible pathways in progression, and appropriate counselling.

Helen Williams, Educational Consultant, Bradford

I believe that every child is gifted and talented. Part of our role as teachers is to provide a range of learning opportunities to enable children to identify their particular gift(s) or talent(s). Further use of this will make them feel good and increase their confidence and self-esteem. This makes them more likely to succeed, break out of their comfort zone and discover a whole range of gifts and talents.

GAT teaching and learning is about allowing each student to reach their full potential by providing them with the skills, resources and opportunities they need to do this. This takes a whole lot of time and energy, building relationships with students and classes and then a fair amount of risk.

My work involves …

- mentoring/coaching teachers
- mentoring students at year 9 and 11
- developing resources to raise standards in schools
- creating schemes of work
- delivering lectures and seminars to trainee teachers.

The biggest challenge for me in this role is …

- empowering people to change.

My greatest success/achievement is …

- building relationships with students and staff.

4. I need ideas for enriching the thinking of my GAT learners

'Thinking' can be pretty slippery when you try to pin it down for a definition. It needs thought, but thankfully we have a word for this: metacognition – thinking about thinking. That's what we'll be doing in this chapter. First of all, I'll offer you frameworks for your metacogitation and then a host of practical ideas for stimulating thinking at all levels and in all curriculum areas. Finally, there are five 'brain bytes': short, focused facts about the brain (and thinking) for direct use with GAT learners.

High-level thinking is strongly associated with GAT learners and is a very helpful characteristic for identifying them. The following ideas will also support their study of particular (and sometimes obsessive) areas of personal interest.

Different ways of thinking about thinking

Experts propose many different definitions and numerous ways to categorise the skills of thinking. Over fifty classifications have been identified by researchers at Newcastle University. One of the best-known and most useful is Bloom's taxonomy. This links to UK National Curriculum requirements and weaves its way into subject-level descriptors – especially in science and DT. It's a useful way to think about thinking. Here's a quick reminder. Use it to help you think about your learners' thinking.

	Bloom's taxonomy: *Typical behaviours*		
Thinking type	*Thinking about ...*	*Asking ...*	*Learners will be ...*
Lower order			
Knowledge	facts	What?, Where?, When?, Who?	finding out
Understanding	relating facts to each other	How do these facts relate to each other?	explaining what they know
Higher order			
Application	using what they know	Where, when and how can I use what I know?	solving problems and meeting challenges
Analysis	breaking ideas down	How can I separate what I know into its important parts?	enquiring and investigating
Synthesis	creating new things and ideas	How can I combine the things I know into something new?	making original things
Evaluation	comparing and judging	How can I decide which is best or worst?	assessing against criteria

The National Curriculum requires the following thinking skills to be developed:

- information processing
- reasoning
- enquiry
- creativity
- evaluation
- metacognition.

It's a list that matches Bloom's taxonomy very closely:

National Curriculum	Bloom
Information processing	Knowledge, understanding
Reasoning	Understanding, analysis
Enquiry	Analysis, understanding
Creativity	Synthesis
Evaluation	Evaluation
Metacognition	Hmmm

I have looked at several other thinking skills classifications, and have created the following table to summarise them. I hope it will help you to understand and develop the thinking of your GAT learners.

Summary of types of thinking

Type of thinking	What it involves	For example
Managing thoughts	Organising, remembering and recalling thoughts	Categorising reasons for the Roman invasion of Britain in AD43, then presenting this in a table
Using thoughts	Applying remembered and organised thoughts in new and diverse situations	Defending the UK presence in Iraq by drawing on historical examples, including the Roman invasion of Britain
Creating thoughts	Having new ideas by combining thoughts in original ways	Producing several realistic alternatives to war and invasion
Thinking about thoughts	Planning, monitoring and evaluating the above	Comparing the process of thinking about invasion to an exemplar model of thinking about conflict (UN conflict management)

All the activities in this book allow learners to get to grips with their specialisms and to understand their own thinking better. Everyone will be able to access the tasks at their own level, but each task offers something specific to GAT learners.

Two powerful thinking tools

1. Hierarchies, heterarchies and elevators

GAT learners get:

- a chance to explore their specialisms/interests in great detail
- the opportunity to develop their knowledge base.

Hierarchy: any system of persons or things ranked one above another
Heterarchy: a network of elements sharing the same horizontal position of power and authority
Elevator: a moving platform or cage for carrying passengers or freight from one level to another

Hierarchies organise things vertically; heterarchies do the same horizontally. For example, think of the way plants and animals have been organised by biologists.

Scientists have both proved and disproved the effectiveness of *Echinacea* in fighting upper-respiratory tract diseases (colds).

Hierarchy: Where *Echinacea* fits in the vertical world of plants	**Heterarchy:** Some of the different species of *Echinacea*
Kingdom: *Plantae* Division: *Magnoliophyta* Class: *Magnoliopsida* Order: *Asterales* Family: *Asteraceae* Tribe: *Heliantheae* Genus: *Echinacea*	*Echinacea angustifolia* – narrow-leaf coneflower *Echinacea atrorubens* – Topeka purple coneflower *Echinacea laevigata* – smooth coneflower, smooth purple coneflower *Echinacea pallida* – pale purple coneflower *Echinacea paradoxa* – yellow coneflower, Bush's purple

This concept of vertical and horizontal classification can be used to think up and down subject matter and then to think across it – and therefore explore all the nooks and crannies. It's a bit like an elevator; you can ride an elevator up and down; you can get off at different floors and walk around; you can then get back on, ride to another floor and explore that one too. It's not a difficult concept, but it's a powerful one when used to structure and expand thinking. You can start with a simple idea, take it higher and lower, then explore it at its different levels.

Manage your thoughts

1. Choose a learning objective.
2. Identify a concept from the learning objective.
3. Put an example of the concept on the middle 'floor'.
4. Identify a way in which this concept can change.

5. Change it 'up', then 'down', by taking it three floors higher and three floors lower in discrete steps – e.g. better as we go up / worse as we go down.
6. At each floor identify three similar concepts.

Use your thoughts

- *Maths* – numbers: more/less; equivalent fractions/percentages on same floor.
- *Language* – authors: more fantasy/real-world; similar author on same floor.
- *Science* – mass: more/less; objects with similar mass on same floor.
- *Geography* – cities: larger/smaller populations; similar populations on same floor.
- *History* – acts from history: good/evil; similar acts on same floor.
- *Music* – instruments' notes: more/less range; similar range on same floor.
- *Art* – artists' work: more/less photographic; similar clarity of image on same floor.
- *PE* – team size: more/fewer players; same team size on same floor.
- *PSHE/RE* – emotions: more/less intense; similar intensity on same floor.
- *DT* – tool danger: higher/lower; similar danger on same floor.
- *MfL* – number of phonemes in language; more/fewer and examples on each floor.

Create new thoughts

- add more floors
- find more equivalent ideas on each floor
- give the elevator a choice of two or more routes up/down
- add ideas between floors
- invent other elevators starting at different parts of a floor and taking ingenious routes.

Example

1. *Choose a learning objective:*
   Understand the environmental impact of different types of transport

2. *Identify a concept from the learning objective*:
   Method of travel

3. *Put an example of the concept on the middle 'floor':*
   Car

4. *Identify a way in which this concept can change*:
   More or less damage to environment

You can create a diagram to present your findings. Here is an example.

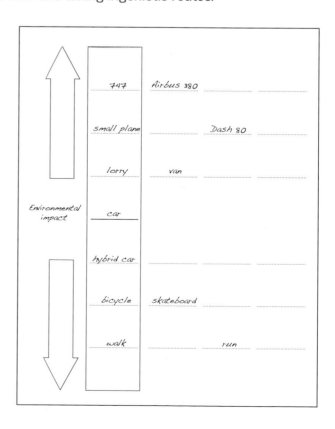

Hierarchies, heterarchies and elevators

     Permission to Photocopy

2. Glass bead thinking

GAT learners get:

- a chance to express their specialisms/interests in great detail
- the opportunity to develop their creative thinking across different subjects
- the opportunity to compete at their intellectual level.

In 1946 Hermann Hesse produced his master work and Nobel prize-winning novel *The Glass Bead Game*. It's a satisfying if lengthy and heavyweight read. It traces the 23rd-century life of Joseph Knecht and describes the kingdom of Castalia, an intellectual paradise into which the world's gifted and talented (male) scholars are shepherded during their teenage years.

The story circles around Castalia's formidable cerebral pursuit, the Glass Bead Game, and Knecht's rise to fame as its Magister Ludi, master of the game. Throughout several hundred pages Hesse provides tantalising glimpses of the game and its rules, though he withholds a definitive description. Part of the book's fascination is in the way in which readers are drawn into creating their own interpretation of the Glass Bead Game.

The game combines logical and creative thinking across different fields of human knowledge, but is centred on musical composition. A 'go' might involve the placing of an idea from mathematics that links to a previously played idea from language or philosophy or science. Each go continues and develops a theme. The game player's skill is vested in his ability to make connections across broad and diverse areas of academic knowledge.

A straightforward interpretation of the Glass Bead Game can easily be constructed by and for GAT learners. It'll help them to make connections between ideas and explore their particular favourite subjects in an alternative and engaging way.

Manage your thoughts

1. Choose a topic, subject or theme.
2. Choose a game board (see examples on page 37).
3. Two to four players take turns to think up and place/write ideas in the empty spaces (on the board, on strips of paper, or using counters/stones/objects to symbolise ideas).
4. All ideas must be directly linked to the chosen theme.
5. As each new idea is placed, a player says how it relates to others to which it is connected by a line.
6. Ideas may be placed in spaces not currently connected to other ideas.
7. Continue until the board is complete, then summarise the thinking that's just taken place.
8. Optionally include points – 1 for every valid idea and 1 for every valid connection.

Use your thoughts

Suggested themes:

- *Maths* – 2D shapes, 3D shapes, areas where maths can be applied, numbers less than 1.
- *Language* – authors, book titles, types of word, letters, poems, languages, characters, plays.
- *Science* – elements, types of force, materials, animals, plants, solids, equipment.
- *Geography* – places, types of transport, services, land use, land features, cities.
- *History* – characters, events, dates, types of evidence, opinions, decades, fashions.
- *Music* – instruments, composers, phrases, timbres, notation, dynamics, record labels, artists.
- *Art* – artists, media, colours, materials, galleries, themes of study, famous works.
- *PE* – sports, personalities, equipment, rules, play areas, scoring systems, laws.
- *PSHE/RE* – emotions, laws, beliefs, holy objects/texts, rights, responsibilities.
- *DT* – tools, customers, design flaws, markets, types of product, historical products.
- *MfL* – useful phrases, native languages, key vocabulary, idiosyncrasies.

Create new thoughts

- invent different boards
- construct 3D boards
- use a chess board or other existing game board
- ideas must be expressed only in symbols, pictures or photos
- ideas must be expressed only in sounds, movements or natural objects
- make the evolving game into a piece of art
- change game rules to include two or more related themes
- change game rules to include two or more random themes
- remove all theme restrictions – anything goes as long as links may be made between ideas
- start with a completed game and deduce the links between ideas
- change the theme halfway through a game
- set time limits for each go or for completion of the game
- decide criteria and judge the quality of ideas and connections
- join two or more boards together.

Example: types of transport

- *Player 1:* car (1 idea = 1 point)
- *Player 2:* hot-air balloon (1 idea = 1 point)
- *Player 1:* plane (1 idea and 2 connections – car and plane have wheels, plane and balloon fly = 3 points)
- *Player 2:* airport monorail (1 idea and 3 connections – monorail and plane both at airport, monorail and balloon both work off the ground, monorail and car both allow passengers a forward view = 4 points)

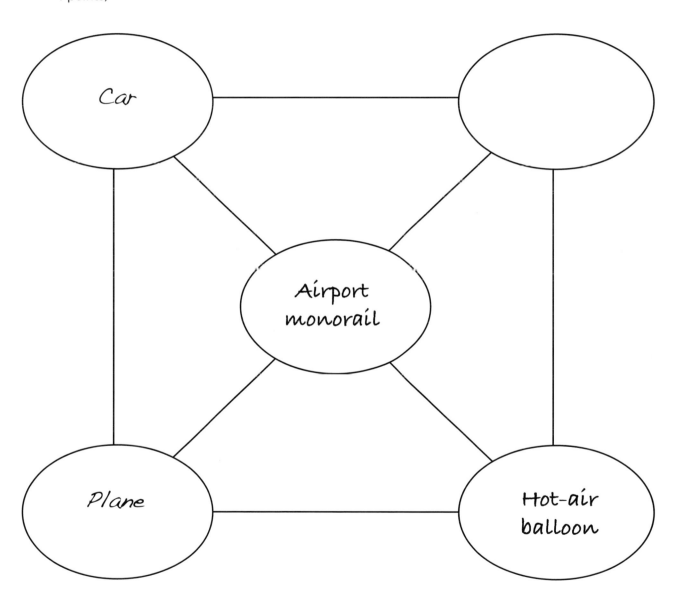

Glass bead thinking

Sample game boards

These are starting points. Create custom boards to suit your GAT learners' needs.

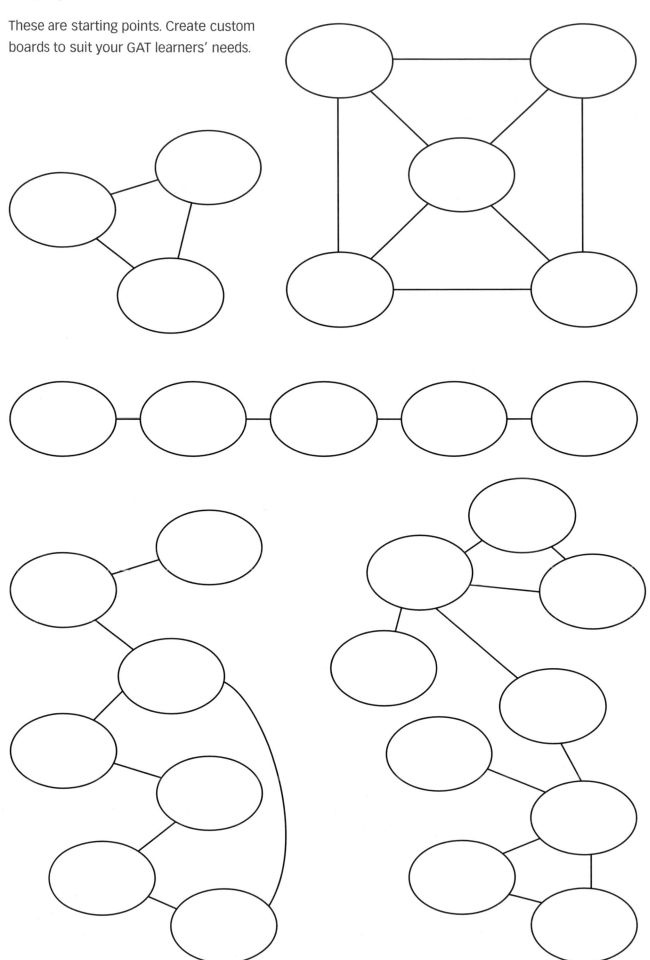

© Including Gifted, Able and Talented Children in the Primary Classroom LDA   Permission to Photocopy

Two creative / visual thinking tools

1. Thinking wall

GAT learners get:

- a chance to express their specialisms/interests in a safe way
- the opportunity to share their expertise with others in a safe way
- the opportunity to develop their creativity.

This activity is especially suited to the inclusive teaching of GAT learners. It allows them to contribute their ideas in a safe and valued way, thereby avoiding the danger of élitist labelling.

Manage your thoughts

A thinking wall is a large blank space onto which words may be written and images and objects stuck. Here are some examples:

- A long strip of lining paper fixed around a classroom or along a corridor.
- An old white sheet pinned to the wall.
- A washing line with pegs strung across a classroom.
- A white-washed playground wall.
- A flipchart page.
- An interactive whiteboard.
- A dry-wipe board.
- A clean dustbin covered with lining paper.
- A big empty book.

The thinking wall may be used in many ways. Here's a straightforward three-part activity:

1. Learners silently contribute their own ideas to the thinking wall.
2. Learners review all contributions made to the thinking wall.
3. Learners select several ideas from the thinking wall and use them to create something new.

Example

1. After some research and reading, learners spend 5 minutes in writing their favourite lines from poems on the thinking wall.
2. Learners take a further 5 minutes to read all the lines that have been added.
3. Learners select eight lines and combine them to create a new poem.

A GAT learner's extensive knowledge and love of eleventh-century troubadour song cycles can anonymously appear on the wall (distinctive handwriting allowing). Someone with no knowledge of poetry can take part too as long as pressure to contribute is not exerted.

Use your thoughts

Here are some suggestions. Remember to choose a theme, a recording method and rules to match the needs and abilities of your learners. A theme may be chosen (secretly) to play to a GAT learner's interests and strengths, without disadvantaging the other children. In fact, it may raise the bar for them. The GAT learners will be able to contribute their ideas to share with all.

- *Maths* – numbers: create real-life problem.
- *Language* – favourite words: create interesting sentences.
- *Science* – pieces of equipment and materials: create an experiment.
- *Geography* – features of a town: create an ideal town.
- *History* – historical characters: create an evil tyrant.
- *Music* – musical phrases: create a melody.
- *Art* – colours in pencil: create a picture limited to four colours.
- *PE* – sports personalities: create a dream team.
- *PSHE/RE* – features of acts of worship: create a new act of worship.
- *DT* – key features of popular consumer products: create an improved product.
- *MfL* – key phrases: create top-ten phrase book.

Create new thoughts

A thinking wall makes creativity visible: existing ideas (contributed by more than one learner) are combined in novel ways to make original pieces. It may be adapted in several ways, thereby altering the creativity process:

- Adjust the time limits for contributions and viewing.
- Remove time limits – encourage contributions over days rather than minutes and let creations emerge when learners are ready (rather than by home time).
- Allow learners to add comments to others' contributions on the wall (agree rules for this).
- Play music during the activity.
- Restrict the form of contributions – photos, drawings, small objects, materials, handwritten text, typed text, symbols, diagrams, sound clips, video clips, actions.
- Pair learners.
- Allow (even insist) on talking while contributing.
- Ask visitors / other learners / parents / wider community to contribute.

2. Creative tracks

GAT learners get help with the process of being creative.

This activity may be used in conjunction with a thinking wall. It's a more structured creativity process that combines a small number of ideas in a formal way. With this small number of ideas, a great many creative combinations emerge. Creative tracks may be a relief to GAT learners who excel in specific knowledge areas, but need help with the more creative aspects of learning and thinking. It takes out the unknown, intuitive aspects of being creative.

Manage your thoughts

A straightforward creative tracks activity requires one starting point, two themes linked to the starting point and five ideas related to the each theme (ten ideas). Both sets of five ideas are arranged on two parallel tracks, next to each other. This makes five pairings. One track is then moved while the other remains fixed. Five new pairings are created as ideas now line up with new partners.

Example

- Starting point: phrases for a fantasy weather poem.
- Theme 1: Adjectives (tepid, crumbling, icy, deafening, sparkling).
- Theme 2: Types of weather (snow, sunshine, thunder, drizzle, storm).

Tepid	Crumbling	Icy	Deafening	Sparkling
Snow	Sunshine	Thunder	Drizzle	Storm

Tepid snow? Deafening drizzle? Are we really in the UK? Let's shift the top track along:

	Tepid	Crumbling	Icy	Deafening	Sparkling
Snow	Sunshine	Thunder	Drizzle	Storm	

We now have Tepid sunshine, Crumbling thunder and Sparkling snow (by letting the end word run round to the beginning).

Moving the tracks backwards and forwards against each other creates twenty-five possible combinations.

Use your thoughts

Here are some suggestions for using creative tracks:

- *Maths* – **Starting point**: Can it be a shape? **Themes**: Number of sides, number of right angles.
- *Language* – **Starting point**: Character descriptions. **Themes**: Adjectives, facial features.
- *Science* – **Starting point**: States of matter. **Themes**: Solids, processes (heating, freezing, etc.).
- *Geography* – **Starting point**: Potential new buildings. **Themes**: Uses of building, types of construction.
- *History* – **Starting point**: Enquiry. **Themes**: Ways of recording events, events worth recording.
- *Music* – **Starting point**: Composition. **Themes**: Instruments, short phrases.
- *Art* – **Starting point**: Sculpture. **Themes**: 3D material, subjects for study.
- *PE* – **Starting point**: Tactics. **Themes**: Shrewd competitive thoughts, sports.
- *PSHE/RE* – **Starting point**: Integration. **Themes**: Ethnic groups, ways of meeting others.
- *DT* – **Starting point**: New shops. **Themes**: Customer groups, product groups.
- *MfL* – **Starting point**: Daily life. **Themes**: Family members, common activities.

Create new thoughts

Creative tracks may be adapted in many ways. As always, do what's right for your learners, and feel free to target any modifications towards your GAT learners:

- Lengthen/shorten the tracks.
- Add more themes and therefore more tracks.
- Instead of tracks have wheels within wheels.

- Instead of tracks have cogs turning against each other.
- Make the tracks from strips of paper/card and fasten their ends together into bands.
- Make the tracks from people – each person is an idea.
- Choose non-obvious or random themes.
- Make new tracks using ideas created from existing tracks.

Real problem-solving

The preceding activities can liven up most lessons and engage all learners with high-order thinking. As these skills develop, they can be brought to bear on imaginative scenarios or real-life situations. Then they really do become thinking tools.

As a young child, a friend of mine had a Winnie-the-Pooh fuzzy-felt set. He used it to imagine that the Blustery Day had turned into a devastating hurricane and destroyed the 100-Aker Wood. He spent many hours trying to construct a dwelling for Pooh and his friends from the remaining felt branches and leaves (green cloud shapes).

He imposed certain criteria on the house. There had to be a room for each character (except Kanga and Roo, who would, of course, share) and there had to be bedding (leaves or fluffy white clouds). This involved endless experimenting with the shape of the house, thoughts about how it could be partitioned and consideration of the equal distribution of bedding.

This is innocent play, but look at the variety of skills that he was quietly developing in this make-believe world – creativity, critical thinking, decision-making, spatial awareness, organisation, evaluation.

Imaginative scenarios can be great vehicles to develop higher-order skills and are a safe introduction to real-life problems.

The activity supplied (page 43) is a fun way to get started which all learners can access, and which provides GAT learners with the chance to excel in creative problem-solving.

BBC Gnome-service News Bulletin

The Department of Eco-gnomics has informed us that, at midnight, the toadstool disease reached catastrophic proportions. Toadstools are disintegrating at an alarming rate, often collapsing into slimy, steaming messes. Our citizens are returning to their gnomadic existence and gnomehomelessness is reaching crisis point.

Aid has been offered by our neighbours, the dwarfs. They are willing to sell us prefabricated building materials called blic-blocs. However, the price of blic-blocs is very 'hi-ho'. Each family will be allocated a certain number of blic-blocs. Due to the crisis, the following rules apply:

- A maximum of 7 blic-blocs per family.

- 1 blic-bloc costs 1 gno-money (about £5000).

- Cost of building on 1 blic-bloc-sized square of land is 1 gno-money.

- For every blic-bloc above two storeys, there is building tax of 1 gno-money.

- Families will be given a grant of 10 gno-moneys to buy their new dwelling.

We understand that the children of your class are excellent problem-solvers. Please help us by designing a new gnome-home. Your designs must be affordable (no more than 10 gno-moneys in total) and stable – they mustn't fall down in high winds or if big people stomp by. They must also give the best value for money – using the largest number of blic-blocs for the cheapest price.

Please present us with plans of the new home (so the builders can reproduce it), a model (made from toy bricks), and a breakdown of the costs.

Gnomon Gnozic   (Gnome Secretary)

Give children the opportunity to work alone or in small groups. In your engagement with them, use these and similar questions to activate higher-order thinking:

- What constitutes best value for money?
- How did you investigate? Systematically or randomly?
- How would you budget a fixed allowance per week?
- What would it feel like to lose your home and all your possessions overnight?
- How does aid work?
- What makes a good building plan?

Extension

The gnomes were in crisis again a few weeks later. Owing to bad weather conditions, a shipment of building materials (large stones, small stones, sand) and food supplies (salt) had met with an accident. The goods had become completely mixed. Can the children separate samples of the mixture and write a comprehensive set of instructions (with easy-to-follow diagrams) to show the gnomes how to do this? Can they also present their ideas and answer questions about the processes used?

Once again working in small groups, the children may use a variety of talents and skills. They will have to:

- apply their scientific knowledge
- share and explore ideas – giving reasons and explanations
- make decisions
- evaluate the success of their work and the quality of their result.

Starting points for scenario problems

Here are four ideas to get you thinking about imaginative scenarios that you may wish to create. I've also suggested related real-world extensions in which your learners could apply their skills. In each case I've highlighted a particular GAT need which is met by the (inclusive) scenario problem.

Imaginative scenarios

GAT learner need	Imaginative scenario problem	Real-world extension
Opportunity to shine in spite of having low self-esteem	The alien race of Fruntles have been blessed with hardly any skills or knowledge about anything at all (apart from interstellar travel). Teach them the one thing that you're best at.	Children share expertise with younger learners or trusted adults, or privately to an imaginary, future audience.
Opportunity to express talents without having to talk or write	An advertising company needs ideas for marketing many different products to customers globally, but wants to use only images and sounds, instead of different languages.	Look at real ad/branding companies and invite them into school to judge learners' work. For examples: www.withsass.com
Opportunity to work and learn with experts who share particular talent	The World Council of [insert talent such as mathematics or sport] is about to be abolished. Its supreme leader wants your help to make the case for saving it.	Invite experts to come in and/or arrange visits related to particular talents and present your imaginary scenario.
Opportunity to develop emotional intelligence and teamwork	Six people are being chosen to start a colony on a newly discovered planet. What skills and talents does your group possess collectively and why should you be chosen to go?	Set teams real challenges such avas: creating publicity materials for the school, organising a learning celebration for parents, building links with the wider community, creating and performing a stage show.

Scenarios do take time to plan and organise, but they can be written to meet GAT-specific and general learning needs. They can be adapted, recycled and reused and often provide several lessons' worth of activity.

Brain bytes

I'll finish up our thinking in this chapter with five brain bytes (see pages 46 and 47). Copy them, cut them out and use them directly with GAT learners to help them understand their brains and value themselves. Each byte provides information and questions to stimulate discussion and debate.

Brain bytes

Brain Byte No. 1: What sort of thinker are you?

Everyone thinks in a slightly different way, but there are two main types of thinking: analytic and holistic. Analytic thinking is logical and takes things one step at a time. Holistic thinking is creative and looks at the big picture. Analytic thinkers like reasons and try to keep things neat and tidy and in order. Holistic thinkers like stories and feelings and try to find the links between things. Their ideas (and work) may be scattered all over the place. Each person has a mixture of these two types of thinking, but usually favours one of them.

- Are you more analytic or holistic?
- Is one type of thinking better or worse than the other?
- What may happen when analytic and holistic thinkers work and learn together?

Brain Byte No. 2: Do you think you are clever?

Everyone thinks something different about being clever. Some people think it's to do with having a high IQ and passing tests. Others believe intelligence is about common sense and solving problems. Some experts even think there are many different ways to be clever. Everyone agrees that being smart has something to do with the brain and how it works, but they can't agree on which bits of the brain are 'clever' and which aren't.

- What is intelligence?
- Can people become cleverer?
- Are you intelligent?

Brain Byte No. 3: How do you think you are clever?

Professor Howard Gardner believes that there are eight different ways to be clever. He tells us that each different 'intelligence' is linked to a different area of the brain. If a certain part of the brain gets damaged, one intelligence suffers while the others don't. This means that some people can sing but not talk, think but not recognise emotions, imagine but not move. Gardner's eight ways to be clever are: musically, with language, with nature, with other people, by yourself, visually, logically, and with your body. He says that each way is just as good as the others. This would mean that a good bit of maths is as valuable as a good tackle or a great poem.

- In which ways are you clever?
- Is everyone clever?
- Is it possible to use different intelligences at the same time?

Brain bytes continued

Brain Byte No. 4: How do you feel?

Your emotions seem to happen in your body, but they begin in your brain. When you sense something, your brain clocks it and then sends signals to your body telling it what to do and which chemicals to make. You then feel something like sadness or frustration or happiness. The part of your brain that looks after emotions is called the limbic system. It's hidden deep in the middle and is made up of bulges and bobbles – like nuts and small fruits. One very interesting part is the amygdala. It fires up if you feel angry and tells your body what to do. But it does this before the rest of your brain gets a chance to think about what's happened.

- Do you always know what you're feeling?
- Is it possible to work out what other people are feeling?
- How can we change what we're feeling?

Brain Byte No. 5: What do you think of yourself?

Professor Carol Dweck has done a lot of work about what people think of themselves. She's found out something really interesting. She's discovered that what you think about yourself can affect how successful you are. She also reckons that what you think about yourself has a lot to do with what other people think of you. She says that some people believe that they can get cleverer and can solve problems – even if it takes a bit of effort. On the other hand, she reckons that some people don't think they can get cleverer and don't think it's worth making the effort if something difficult comes along. Both types of people could solve the problem if they wanted to – but what they believe decides whether they will or won't.

- What do you do when you face a difficult problem?
- What do you believe about yourself and your skills?
- What do other people expect of you?

Gifts and talents don't always come for free. Sometimes there is an emotional cost. By definition GAT learners are different. They may be particularly liable to suffer isolation and bullying. If their learning needs aren't met they may express that deficiency through misbehaviour. In this chapter I shall describe social and emotional challenges faced by GAT learners, then consider how we can support them.

Emma's story

As befits a chapter on emotions, let's start with a powerful story. Emma has recently graduated from university. Her gifts lie in music and languages and she's busy planning both her career and her marriage. Learning for Emma has not always been intellectually enlightening. Empathy is a good start for helping your GAT learners to manage their emotions. If you really know how it feels to feel what they do, then support can be both genuine and effective. So, settle in, suspend judgement, and read Emma's tale.

Reception: I learned to read and write before school. In primary school, we were each paired up with an older child in the class, and I sat one day watching my partner laboriously writing her name. She got as far as the M in her surname before she was called away to the teacher. I looked at the paper, and added the small c that I knew followed the M. When she got back, she praised me extravagantly for being so clever. Even then I knew it was safer to add the next letter rather than the whole name.

Year 2: I had a teacher I loved, who quickly saw that my reading at least was well above average. One day she left the class with a student teacher and took me on my own to the school office, where we sat on the floor together with a pile of books. She got me to read passages from each of them. From then on, I was sent to the next class up to choose my reading books, and occasionally I was given the run of the entire school library.

Year 3: The teacher seemed to take an instant dislike to me. She put me back onto the reading-scheme books that I had finished with. I felt utterly humiliated – I could barely choke out the words when I had to read to her.

The class was for both year 3 and year 4, so two sets of spellings were put up on the board each time. I found spelling easy, so I would copy down my own words as fast as I could, and then copy the joined-up words meant for year 4 into the back of my exercise book. After a week or two, the teacher realised what I was doing. Every time she would rub the spellings off the board before I had finished.

Year 4: As I was the eldest child in my family, my parents didn't have anyone to compare me to. They had an inkling that I might be above average. When they asked my class teacher, they were informed 'There's nothing special about Emma, she's just average.' Nevertheless, in year 4 they pushed for me to be moved up a year, and in the final term I was transferred to the next class. By the time my parents realised that the move was only temporary, it seemed to be too late to do anything.

That term with the year-5 class was, by and large, a happy and fulfilling time. There was some bullying – but as the child of the parish priest I had stood out for years. I was happy with the work and enjoyed being with older children.

Year 5: The class I had spent the last term with moved up to the next class, while my old year group joined me. Suddenly I was an outsider again, and those of my age regarded me with suspicion. I was badly bullied for the rest of my time at primary school.

Secondary school: The local secondary school had a reputation for being rough, so my parents and I chose a school about twelve miles away. It should have been a new beginning, but my confidence was shattered and I struggled to make friends.

I very quickly got used to being bored in secondary school. In maths we worked individually through booklets, each of which had to be marked by the teacher before we were allowed to go on to the next one. It was possible to spend half or more of a lesson waiting to have work marked. After several weeks of this, I gave up.

In French there was no provision at all for the few who had already learned some in primary school. Two of us were sent on a residential weekend for 'able children'. I thrived in the unashamedly academic atmosphere – and the school did nothing to follow it up.

In year 9, I started to learn German. I rapidly outstripped the rest of the class but had to wait for them to catch up. In a parents' evening, my parents expressed some concerns that I wasn't being challenged enough in class, and were informed that 'Emma's memory won't always be so good, you know. It will deteriorate.'

Throughout secondary school I encountered many teachers who seemed intimidated by my intelligence and resented my enthusiasm to learn more than the minimum prescribed.

As I became more miserable at school, I became frequently ill and was often absent. By the beginning of year 11, the stress of being constantly frustrated academically and rejected socially had taken its toll, and I became ill with what was later diagnosed as ME. It removed me from a situation that had become unbearable. I spent the rest of the year getting better.

College: The following year I started GCSE courses at the local sixth-form college, where I gradually rebuilt my confidence and learned to make friends. I was almost never bored. After achieving what was apparently the highest GCSE score of any student at that college in seven subjects, I started A-level courses in English literature, music and German. After a year at the college I had relaxed into an informal, equal attitude towards my teachers and I found that they encouraged me and appreciated my interest. Only in my tutorial subject, German, did I encounter problems. After a long struggle, the head of department supported my request to be moved to a more challenging tutorial group. I was exultant at having finally stood up for myself.

University: I was allowed to take a certain number of classes outside my official degree subject, music, and I found myself in a second-year German class, where my marks rarely dropped below a first. Another first-year music student was in the same class and we became close friends. In our second year our stage-5 class had disappeared abroad and we were in a class of finalists. Problems quickly became apparent, despite our attempts to make friends with the new group. None had the confidence to answer questions in class, and the main lecturer (new that year) seemed unsure how to cope. We were asked to take a back seat in class, to give the others a chance to come forward. The effect was devastating for both of us. By the end of the year I couldn't bring myself to go to the German lectures, and my friend had panic attacks in her exams and did badly. In our final year she had a massive panic attack in an exam.

My life of learning: I still blame myself for my problems in school. I cannot forgive myself for not standing up for myself more.

You will have noticed many powerful and important themes running through Emma's educational life. Although she is very hard on herself, she demonstrates an additional gift not formally recognised during her school life – the gift of emotional intelligence.

Emotional intelligence

A definition of 'e-motion' is 'the drawing out of an action'. Emotions trigger us to respond. If we are frightened, we run (or fight or negotiate). Happiness is a call to celebrate and disgust is the stimulus to wrinkle our noses and move on. Sometimes we choose not to respond to our emotions. This may be right (if we feel we want to 'educate' a child physically) or harmful (if we cower to a bully).

Emotional intelligence involves the awareness and management of our emotional lives, and our ability to form and maintain relationships. Michael Fullan, an expert in educational change, defines it as 'the ability to work effectively with people you don't like'. The truth is in there.

The concept was first introduced by Charles Darwin in 1872, but waited over a hundred years to be popularised by Daniel Goleman. It's now a major strand in the development of any organisation that recognises its people as key to success.

Aptitude in emotional intelligence comprises several distinct abilities:

1. Perception

   Recognising and naming the emotions of yourself, others and groups

2. Management

   Awareness of your emotional abilities – strength and weaknesses
   Application of your emotions – choosing to act or choosing not to act
   Evaluation – of your emotions and their associated actions

3. Expression

   Showing your emotions to the right people and in the right way.

Emma's story serves two purposes: firstly, to help us understand the emotional challenges faced by GAT learners; secondly, to show us what emotional intelligence in action looks like.

Staff development activity

Find examples from Emma's story to illustrate each element of emotional intelligence.

Emotional challenges for GAT learners

Emma's story highlights many of the potential difficulties for GAT learners. However, we need to consider each learner separately and avoid stereotyping (identifying the boisterous and frustrated sporting genius and the geeky and withdrawn mathematical mastermind). Many GAT children do sail through school without any additional emotional challenges.

B.A. Bracken and E.F. Brown studied forty-five gifted students and forty-five without any identified gift, and asked teachers to rate all ninety on the Clinical Assessment of Behavior (CAB) scale, a measure of behavioural problems. The gifted students scored significantly higher on three scales: Competence, Executive function, and Gifted and talented. Interestingly, they also scored significantly lower on Anxiety, Depression, Attention deficit, Learning disability, Autistic spectrum and Mental retardation, as well as on the total scale score. The results indicated that GAT students displayed overall better behavioural adjustment than their peers. ('Behavioral Identification and Assessment of Gifted and Talented students', *Journal of Psychoeducational Assessment*, Vol. 24, No. 2, 112–122, 2006)

When GAT learners do face difficulties, they're likely to show up as one or more of the following.

Isolation: Learners may find themselves actively isolated (excluded and bullied – by peers or by teachers) or passively isolated (lonely). The first occurs when a social group feels threatened by the GAT learner and consequently rejects them. The second isolation takes place when the learner has no intellectual or interested peers to trust and talk to. There are no like-mindeds around.

Isolation may cause learners to play down their abilities in order to fit in and be accepted. They will turn their gifts towards survival and acceptance: if they appear more like the others then maybe the others will acknowledge them.

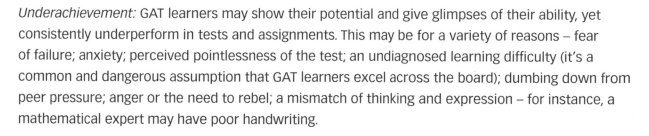

Perfectionism: GAT learners may set extremely high standards for themselves or have them set by others. They know that they're ahead of the game, so why not set the stakes higher? Problems come if their bodies and minds are not yet ready to achieve them.

In 1978, D.E. Hamachek identified six indicators associated with perfectionism: depression, a nagging 'I should' feeling, shame/guilt feelings, face-saving behaviour, shyness/procrastination and self-deprecation. These in themselves provide an interesting potential checklist for GAT learners, though they should not be used exclusively to identify them (*Encounters with the Self*, New York: Holt, Rinehart & Winston).

Underachievement: GAT learners may show their potential and give glimpses of their ability, yet consistently underperform in tests and assignments. This may be for a variety of reasons – fear of failure; anxiety; perceived pointlessness of the test; an undiagnosed learning difficulty (it's a common and dangerous assumption that GAT learners excel across the board); dumbing down from peer pressure; anger or the need to rebel; a mismatch of thinking and expression – for instance, a mathematical expert may have poor handwriting.

You'll see that the three characteristics above are linked and related. For example, a learner who feels unable to meet their own high standards may become isolated from others because of striving to be the best, and may then underachieve as a means to gain reacceptance in the group.

The emotional needs of GAT learners may be complex and need to be addressed. The energy they expend on dealing with negative feelings is energy diverted from learning. But it's not just the GAT learners for whom you need to look out. All learners have a rich and vulnerable emotional life and any support you provide to one group could and should be offered to everyone.

Emotional support for GAT learners

There are four overlapping approaches to supporting your GAT learners:

- Develop your own emotional intelligence.
- Teach emotional intelligence to your learners.
- Build effective relationships with your GAT learners.
- Facilitate effective relationships between all learners.

Here's a small collection of practical ways to do this.

Circle time: Jenny Mosley is a stalwart of the primary classroom. In her Quality Circle Time model, sitting in a circle symbolises equality. Every learner (GAT or not) has equal rights and responsibilities to contribute to class discussions, celebrations and solutions. This is a tool for building a strong community of learners and for valuing each person in the community.

One topic of discussion could be 'What do you do best?' If each learner is able to share a talent, GAT learners achieve two things: valuing and acceptance of their abilities, and reduction in the likelihood of isolation (if potential bullies feel valued, their noses are less likely to be pushed out of joint).

Cool-to-be-clever culture: One of the biggest problems faced by GAT learners is that of being seen to be different. Groups notice difference and don't always respond well. GAT learners may be tempted to reduce the difference by making themselves more like everyone else. The problem stems from whether it's OK to do well. Schools do a great job at fostering many forms of achievement, and this in turn creates an ethos in which it's normal to achieve and to try your best. If a cool-to-be-clever culture can be established, GAT differences are no longer marked or unusual.

It's important to include everyone in the ethos, otherwise we simply create another group who are the different ones. Gardner's Multiple Intelligences (MI) theory is an excellent way to develop a cool-to-be-clever culture. Learners can be valued in eight different ways (the eight intelligences). If these strengths are publicly esteemed (in a display, for example), everyone has displayed evidence that they are clever.

Circle of friends: The circle of friends involves GAT learners meeting together with expert teacher facilitation on a regular basis – maybe once a week or once a fortnight. They get to meet like-minded people and have a chance to discuss the challenges that they face. Between meetings the circle of friends acts as a support group – just seeing familiar faces around the school may lift a difficult day.

Mentoring: In a mentoring scheme older GAT learners support younger ones. Here's an example.

Hannah, age 18

Hannah has just finished her A-level exams, and after a well-earned summer break will be off (grades willing, fingers crossed) to university to study religion, philosophy and ethics. In the sixth form, she has taken on social responsibilities and organised fund-raising events. She's also been a GAT mentor to younger students.

After GCSEs she was herself identified as GAT by her English and RE teachers and asked, with others, to take part in the mentoring programme. After a day's training Hannah was teamed up with four GAT year-7 students, and over the following term she spent several afternoons with them. They worked on a range of topics including learning skills, learning styles and teamwork. From then on Hannah made herself available to meet her four students informally and as they needed her. This ranged from a simple greeting to short meetings after school or in tutor time. Hannah says:

When they come up from the primary schools, some of these bright children want to hide their talents. They don't want to stand out as being clever in case they get picked on. What we have to do is be positive role models and show them that it's cool to be clever. We're a lot older than them and we're in the sixth form so they look up to us. It might not work so well if the mentors were nearer their age. We did some sessions with them to help them with their learning and social skills, and then whenever we saw them around school we made a point of saying 'Hello'.

I reckon it's a good idea to look after the gifted year 7s like this because they have someone older who knows how they feel and whom they can trust. It gives them some confidence that it's OK to be bright and someone will stand up for them. It's also good for me to put on my UCAS form!

But I think that the school should give this sort of thing to all of the year 7s. I suppose really it's not the gifted ones who need it the most. We could do learning styles with the children who aren't doing so well and maybe they would get on a bit better.

I was never Gifted and Talented in my primary school and I've never wanted to hide what I'm good at. In the sixth form everybody just got on with things. We sort of knew who was good at what even if it wasn't something really academic. Because we all had something we were good at no one was left out.

This GAT mentoring model is an interesting one to explore for KS1 and KS2. It could take several forms: year 2s working with year Rs and year 6s with year 3s in a teacher-led programme of learning skills, social skills, thinking skills and individual project work. The real benefit of a GAT mentoring scheme is its effect on the esteem of the GAT learners who feel able to share and celebrate their gifts rather than hiding them.

GAT learners face unique emotional challenges, but we have the tools to meet those. It's a great start simply to be aware of the problems they may encounter. Any solutions that you choose will benefit everyone in the class.

GAT learners in the twenty-first century

Here's a sobering thought. In 2003, Jim O'Neill, a global economist for the Goldman Sachs investment bank, proposed the BRIC Thesis. He suggested that by 2050 the four principal economic powers will be Brazil, Russia, India and China. By then these countries are predicted to account for 40 per cent of the world's population and to hold a combined GDP of nearly 15 trillion dollars. Add to this the words of Stan Shih, entrepreneur and pioneer of Taiwan's electronics industry, 'The effective development of brainpower in a nation will decide the prosperity of the country in the future', and you'll see why it's vital to provide curricula that:

- give all learners the skills and knowledge to survive and succeed in a changing world;
- identify, value and extend the best learners in their particular areas of expertise.

If we want to stay ahead as a nation, we need to find, nurture and utilise our best minds.

Curricula must prepare children for the future and be flexible enough to evolve with not only global trends but also more localised needs. For example, the English secondary curriculum now includes financial management in response to the growing problem of adult debt. Curricula should also be deep enough and wide enough to harness the enthusiasm and specialisms of GAT learners – specialisms that will play a major part in this century's success. Governments have responded to the global educational challenge. Here are two similar approaches, initiated in 2003:

Every Child Matters – England	*A Curriculum for Excellence – Scotland*
Every child has the support they need to: Enjoy and achieve Stay safe Be healthy Make a positive contribution Achieve economic well-being	To enable all young people to become: Successful learners Confident individuals Responsible citizens Effective contributors

Top-level requirements like these have an impact on the design and delivery of curricula. Achievement nowadays relies on skills as well as knowledge, and learners need the opportunity to develop a range of competencies and behaviours alongside their acquisition of facts.

Customised curricula

Also in 2003, the Secretary of State for education launched Excellence and Enjoyment, a national strategy and educational vision in which 'high standards are obtained through a rich, varied and exciting curriculum which develops children in a range of ways'. After many years of tight curriculum control, the government have let go of the reins just a little. Schools now have freedom, within limits, to create a curriculum that meets the needs of their children and the global market more closely. They are encouraged to innovate and to develop a curriculum with distinctive character. This is a wonderful opportunity to plan in experiences and opportunities for GAT learners.

There are many stakeholders in a primary school's curriculum – children, teachers, parents, governors, feeder secondary schools, future employers and wider society.

In addition, there are numerous factors that try to shape it: political agendas, environmental concerns, future economic prosperity, national identity, multi-cultural issues and desirable historical perspectives, for instance. The needs of GAT learners are important, but they are part of all of these. We must be realistic and practical as we attempt to enrich the curriculum to support their needs. This means tweaking rather than rewriting.

A curriculum for GAT learners

The National Curriculum in England (2008) looks something like this.

Early learning goals	KS 1 and 2 subjects
Knowledge and understanding of the world Creative development Physical development Personal, social and emotional development Communication, language and literacy Mathematical development	English, Mathematics, Science, Design and technology, Information and communication technology, History, Geography, Art and design, Music, Physical education, Religious education, PSHE and citizenship, a modern foreign language

If a child's gift, talent or special ability lies in one or more of these areas, they are on the agenda. But what if they are a gifted thinker, talented creative problem-solver, able leader or superb team worker?

As yet there is no formal requirement to include skills such as critical thinking, leadership, creativity and collaboration in a primary-school curriculum. Nor is it statutory to address behaviours like risk-taking, self-motivation, determination and empathy. It's up to the individual school.

Many now recognise the need to tackle these areas and do so through PSHE and citizenship or by developing a skills-based curriculum (e.g. the critical skills programme www.criticalskills.co.uk). In these schools, skills and behaviours are developed through the delivery of subject content, not as an addition to it.

In summary, a curriculum includes two things: what to teach and how to teach it.

We'll now look at these two areas from a GAT perspective.

What to teach

In Chapter 1 I presented a generic, customisable definition of GAT learners:

GAT learners are those who do, or could do, something of value much better than others.

The bottom line for curriculum design is that it must reflect your definition of GAT learners. If you've decided that they are the linguists, mathematicians, artists, sports people and academics, then your curriculum must include the teaching and development of these areas. If they are thinkers, creators, leaders and empathisers, then the curriculum should embrace those areas as well. The curriculum should be primed, ready and waiting for any of the gifts, talents and abilities that the school values, should they come along.

Activity: Perform a quick matching exercise

- Place your school's definition of GAT learners next to a summary of the school's curriculum.
- Think about how well they match.
- Does the curriculum provide opportunities for GAT learners to demonstrate and develop their skills?
- Does the curriculum need to change?
- Does the definition of GAT need to change?

I once worked with a school that had extended its definition of GAT learners to include 'Children who give wacky, off-the-wall answers in class.' It was a brilliant idea, but at the time there was no provision in the curriculum to make the wacky answers appear and then apply this creative, imaginative thinking. The talent was identified but not nurtured or used. Here's a solution to that:

- Start at least one lesson a week with a 'What if?' question – linked to the lesson objective.
- Set lateral-thinking problems to be done during register time.
- As part of the end-of-term review set a challenge to find the best question asked in the term.

How to teach

Carolyn Shields researched the performance and attitudes of exceptional fifth-grade students over an academic year. She included those who learned in classes made up of gifted students only and those who learned in mixed classes. At the beginning of the year both sets of GAT learners were about equal. By the end of the year, the first group showed better:

- academic self-concept
- independent development
- self-acceptance
- belief in teachers' reinforcement of student self-concept
- peer relations
- understanding
- intelligence
- reading
- cognition
- metacognition.

Carolyn M. Shields, 'To Group or not to Group Academically Talented or Gifted Students?' *Educational Administration Quarterly*, Vol. 32, No. 2, 295–323 (1996)

One of the biggest debates around GAT learners is whether or not to teach them alongside other pupils. The national trend towards inclusion (of all learners) relies on 'personalised learning' as one technique to achieve this. If all learners are fully understood, and their unique preferences and strengths are taken into account, there's no reason why they can't all learn in the same room. It's good theory, but in practice personalised learning presents many challenges. For example, GAT learners may really stretch the differentiation of content and teacher knowledge. And if their needs aren't met, they may present you with some interesting behaviour.

Do you remember Ruth Lawrence? In 1985, aged 13, she became Oxford University's youngest graduate, achieving a first-class honours degree in mathematics. The child prodigy caught the world's attention and her education came under the spotlight:

Lawrence's amazing ability has been nurtured by her father Harry and her mother Sylvia. A onetime computer consultant, Harry quit work in 1977 to concentrate on making prodigies of the girl and her younger sister Rebecca. Neither child has ever been to school. All their primary and secondary learning has come from Harry and Sylvia, at desks set up in the family kitchen in Huddersfield, Yorkshire.

Partly as a result of this cozy tutorial, Ruth passed her [A-level] exams at nine … Ruth has astounded the faculty at St Hugh's [at Oxford] with the range of her intellect and the ease with which she masters subjects. In one seminar, while other students were struggling with a complex theorem that an academician was elaborating on a blackboard, Lawrence pointed out an error that the lecturer had made. She raced through Oxford's three-year course in two years.

Time Magazine, 5 August, 1985

Professor Ruth Lawrence-Naimark now works at the Albert Einstein Institute of Mathematics, Hebrew University, Jerusalem, specialising in knot theory and topology. Her phenomenal early learning success was clearly partly dependent on exclusion from the standard school experience. How would she have fared in a 1990s numeracy lesson? And how is the next Ruth Lawrence currently being taught?

You will need to make well-judged professional decisions about what is best for each of your GAT learners. It may be preferable for the most exceptionally talented to learn outside the classroom. Consider the pros and cons of different learning options:

- in another year group
- with learners of similar ability/interest (same school)
- with learners of similar ability/interest (at another school)
- at a teachers' professional development centre
- at a local university or college
- at a secondary school
- at home
- in a local business.

Activity: Teach Akrit Jaswal

Imagine that Akrit, at age 7, has just joined year 3 in your school. How would you and your staff meet his needs and ensure that he thrives?

Akrit came to public attention when in 2000 he performed his first medical procedure at his family home. He was seven. His patient – a local girl who could not afford a doctor – was eight. Her hand had been burnt in a fire, causing her fingers to close into a tight fist that wouldn't open. Akrit had no formal medical training and no experience of surgery, yet he managed to free her fingers.

I ask him how he managed to carry out the procedure; wasn't he nervous? 'No, I wasn't. I have read many medical books and attended many operations. I think I did a better job than most surgeons. They would have opted for plastic surgery, but I didn't need to.'

The Times, 4 December 2005

Akrit Jaswal is Indian and grew up in a rural village. He showed an exceptional gift for languages ... began devouring medical textbooks in English and performed his first operation at the age of 7. His knowledge grew such that local doctors began consulting him as their local expert. Needless to say this did not remain unnoticed and at only 12 years old he began studying medicine at university.

www.teamfocus.co.uk

Curriculum enrichment: expert support packs

To help you develop your curriculum for GAT learners, twenty-five expert support packs are offered. Each pack includes ideas and resources for a particular GAT specialism.

What the packs comprise

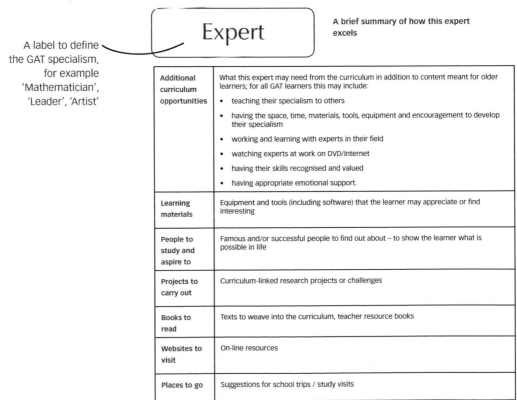

A label to define the GAT specialism, for example 'Mathematician', 'Leader', 'Artist'

Expert

A brief summary of how this expert excels

Additional curriculum opportunities	What this expert may need from the curriculum in addition to content meant for older learners; for all GAT learners this may include: • teaching their specialism to others • having the space, time, materials, tools, equipment and encouragement to develop their specialism • working and learning with experts in their field • watching experts at work on DVD/Internet • having their skills recognised and valued • having appropriate emotional support.
Learning materials	Equipment and tools (including software) that the learner may appreciate or find interesting
People to study and aspire to	Famous and/or successful people to find out about – to show the learner what is possible in life
Projects to carry out	Curriculum-linked research projects or challenges
Books to read	Texts to weave into the curriculum, teacher resource books
Websites to visit	On-line resources
Places to go	Suggestions for school trips / study visits

The packs supply starting points to help you understand, stimulate and extend GAT learners, whilst not excluding the other children. Some of the ideas are for the learners, some are for you. The philosophy underneath this approach is 'The mantle of the expert', in which children are cast in the role of adult experts investigating and becoming specialists in an area.

Visit www.mantleoftheexpert.com for further information, articles and planning.

The packs that follow aren't intended to list every resource going. They provide carefully chosen examples of what's around in order to inspire you. The idea is that you choose only those suggestions that are achievable and relevant to your curriculum. For example, if you've found out that your curriculum does not yet meet the needs of children who excel in questioning skills (see page 61), then you could do one or more of the following:

- include the recommended books in literacy teaching
- include a study of one of the role models during history or PSHE
- read around the subject yourself
- provide the project as an optional homework task
- list the websites for exploration during ICT
- publicly praise questioning skills at assembly time.

Feel free to add to the support packs and create extra ones in the same format. And if you do, it would be kind of you to share them on the GAT discussion boards at www.thinkingclassroom.co.uk

Mathematician

Excels in mathematical understanding and logical/critical/analytic thinking

Additional curriculum opportunities	Carry out extended mathematical investigations Create and solve own puzzles and problems Work with practising mathematicians Prepare a case and argue a point with intellectual peers Use mathematical thinking in other subjects, e.g. flow-charts in literacy
Learning materials	Flow-chart, scientific calculator, old mechanical calculating machines (http://www.nzeldes.com/HOC/HOC_Core.htm is a fascinating history of calculating machines) Zoombinis Maths Journey (GSP Software); Inspiration/Kidspiration (Inspiration Software Inc.) http://www.topmarks.co.uk/Interactive.aspx (free interactive whiteboard resources)
People to study and aspire to	Stephen Hawking (astrophysicist) Isaac Newton (father of modern science) John Forbes Nash (watch *A Beautiful Mind* – cert. 12 – Russell Crowe plays the brilliant but troubled American maths genius)
Projects to carry out	Investigate Boolean algebra and logic gates (http://www.allaboutcircuits.com/vol_4/chpt_7/2.html)
Books to read	*Brain Academy Maths* (Rising Stars Publishing, http://www.risingstars-uk.com)
Websites to visit	http://www.figurethis.org (Intriguing maths challenges) http://mathworld.wolfram.com (take a peek into the world of high-level maths)
Places to go	Royal Institution, London (http://www.rigb.org/rimain/events/programmeformaths_primary.jsp – mathematics masterclasses) Bletchley Park, Milton Keynes (World War 2 cryptography HQ and workplace of mathematician Alan Turing) Murder Mystery at the Beamish Museum, County Durham

Questioner

Excels in curiosity, persistence and determination to find things out using higher- and lower-order questions and/or ability to ask off-the-wall questions

Additional curriculum opportunities	Have enough time to ask questions in all subject areas Have access to individuals who have the time and ability to respond Be exposed to a range of questions: what, which, when, where, who, how, why, what if, why not
Learning materials	Notebook or digital voice recorder to preserve questions and answers
People to study and aspire to	John Humphries Michael Parkinson Libby Purves
Projects to carry out	Create a list of 100 useful questions Investigate what the world's best question might be Extend to different curriculum areas: the world's best mathematical question, artistic question or geographical question
Books to read	*The Little Book of Thunks* by Ian Gilbert (260 questions to make your brain go ouch; Crown House, 2007) *Snowflake Bentley* by Jacqueline Briggs Martin (Houghton Mifflin, 1998) Resource: *Questioning in the Primary School* by Ted Wragg and George Brown (RoutledgeFalmer, 2001)
Websites to visit	http://iws.ccccd.edu/mbrooks/demos/fermi_questions.htm (Fermi problems – fun, real-world questions that rely on making assumptions and estimating large quantities – e.g. How many hairs are there on your head?) http://www.rcls.org/ksearch.htm (a list of child-friendly search engines)
Places to go	Williamson's Tunnels, Liverpool (What are they for? Debate surrounds their actual purpose and questions remain unanswered.) Pitt Rivers Museum, Oxford (mysterious objects from around the world – arranged by type rather than region or historical period) Find a folly – http://www.follytowers.com/ (question the purpose of these curious buildings)

Artist

Excels in visual perception and the creation of original artworks

Additional curriculum opportunities	Explore a wide range of works by different artists in various media Work with practising artists Have time and resources to tackle extended pieces in chosen style/media Have opportunities to enter art competitions Demonstrate learning through visual methods
Learning materials	Access to a wider than normal range of media and tools Revelation Natural Art (Logotron – www.logo.com)
People to study and aspire to	Contemporary artists (try http://www.modernartistsgallery.com/artists.php) Dante Gabriel Rossetti Georges Seurat Damien Hirst
Projects to carry out	Make an exact copy of a well-known work of art Use art skills to represent music, text, natural sounds
Books to read	*Learning to Look at Paintings* by Mary Acton (Routledge, 1997) *99 Ways to Tell a Story* by Matt Madden (Jonathan Cape, 2006) *Manga for Dummies* by Kensuke Okabayashi (Wiley, 2007)
Websites to visit	http://www.kids101-art.co.uk/ (a virtual gallery for schools) http://artmagick.com/ (virtual gallery of obscure nineteenth-century artists) http://www.nga.gov/kids/kids.htm (interactive exhibits from Washington's National Gallery of Art) http://www.nationalgallery.org.uk/education/ (teachers' resources) http://www.growminds.com/TheArts/GTinArt.htm (thinking around young, gifted artists)
Places to go	Courtauld Institute of Art, London Scottish National Gallery of Modern Art, Edinburgh Cumberland Pencil Museum, Keswick Local art galleries

Scientist

Excels in ability to explore the world using scientific methods – asking questions, making hypotheses, testing and then forming new questions

Additional curriculum opportunities	Carry out unconventional experiments Be able to follow own lines of scientific enquiry and interest Work with practising scientists Argue about scientific truth
Learning materials	Extended range of measuring instruments http://www.brightminds.co.uk (navigate to 'Science') Chemistry set Cambridge Brainbox Electronics Kit
People to study and aspire to	Susan Greenfield (neuroscientist) Richard Dawkins (evolutionary biologist) Albert Einstein (physicist) Diane France (forensic anthropologist)
Projects to carry out	Create hypothesis, then plan original (and safe) science experiments to test it out Find out what the most important science questions in the world are right now
Books to read	*Vacuum Bazookas, Electric Rainbow Jelly and 27 Other Saturday Science Projects* by Neil A. Downie (Princeton University Press, 2001) *Brain Academy Science* (Rising Stars Publishing, http://www.risingstars-uk.com) *Focus Magazine* from the BBC (Science and Technology made friendly)
Websites to visit	http://www.sciencedays.org/curriculum/lessons.html (lesson plans) http://www.bbc.co.uk/sn/ (BBC Science and Nature) http://www.techniquest.org/virtual/ (virtual exhibits from Cardiff's Techniquest) http://www.cogsci.uci.edu/personnel/hoffman/vi6.html (intriguing visual experiments)
Places to go	Science Museum, London Eureka – The museum for children, Halifax (Hands on Science) Glasgow Science Centre Dana Centre, London (science café and pop-science events)

Naturalist

Excels in understanding the natural world (plants, animals, natural features and systems); how it fits together and how to care for it

Additional curriculum opportunities	Get involved with local and national conservation projects and campaigns Work with practising naturalists/conservationists Spend extended time in learning outdoors Investigate own special interest in the natural world
Learning materials	Bug-hunting kit Microscope Identification guides – birds, trees, animals, plants, seashore life, etc.)
People to study and aspire to	Amy Vedder (wildlife biologist) Jonathon Porritt (expert on sustainable development) James Lovelock (originator of the Gaia hypothesis) David Bellamy (botanist)
Projects to carry out	Create own taxonomies/hierarchies of plant/animal life Plan and run a campaign to improve the local environment in some way Acquire and look after an exotic (legal) animal
Books to read	*The Blue Planet* by Andrew Byatt *et al*. (BBC Books, 2001) *Superkids: 250 Incredible Ways for Kids to Save the Planet* by Sasha Norris *et al*. (Think Publishing Ltd, 2005) *A Dictionary of Animal Behaviour* by David McFarland (Oxford University Press, 2006)
Websites to visit	http://www.wearewhatwedo.org/ (simple ideas for changing the world) http://www.newscientist.com/blog/environment/index.html (environmental blog) http://www.carbonfootprint.com/ (help save the planet)
Places to go	John Moore Countryside Museum, Tewkesbury Natural History Museum, London Horniman Museum and Gardens, London (collections to inspire understanding of the world's different peoples, cultures and environments) Eden Project, Cornwall

Builder

Excels in the manual construction of small-scale and/or large-scale objects

Additional curriculum opportunities	Build models and dioramas as assessment of learning Work with practising builders / architects / civil engineers Have access to a wide range of building materials and construction kits Have time to construct own models and physical representations
Learning materials	Lego®, Geomag®, Meccano®, Zoobs®, Gears®, etc. Clay, straws, wood, cardboard, sticky tape, string, glue, scissors, etc.
People to study and aspire to	Daniel Liebeskind (architect) Sir Robert McAlpine ('concrete Bob') Mary Maclachlan (senior model maker at WETA model workshop)
Projects to carry out	Construct a scale model of the school
Books to read	*Let's Look at Diggers* (DVD, http://www.jcbshop.com/) *Architecture* (Eyewitness Companion Guide) by Jonanthan Glancey (Dorling Kindersley, 2006) *Spectacular Vernacular: London's 100 Most Extraordinary Buildings* by David Long (Sutton Publishing Ltd, 2006)
Websites to visit	http://en.wikipedia.org/wiki/Scale_model http://www.airfix.com/ http://www.jcb.co.uk/products/MachineRange.aspx (diggers and trucks)
Places to go	Legoland, Windsor Diggerland, Devon, Durham, Kent and Yorkshire CUBE, Liverpool (Centre for the Urban Built Environment) Bursledon Brickworks, Hampshire Local building sites

Entertainer

Excels in the ability to hold an audience's attention and to entertain its members with a variety of content

Additional curriculum opportunities	Present in front of a wide range of audiences – different sizes, ages and ones that are not so easy to please Demonstrate learning through verbal presentation and role play Work with practising entertainers / actors and actresses Have time to prepare and rehearse performances
Learning materials	Puppets Masks Hats Costumes Microphone and sound system (stage and audience) Camcorder and video-editing software
People to study and aspire to	Darcey Bussell (dancer, actress and author) Bono (singer and political activist) Anne Foy (CBBC presenter and actress) Dakota Fanning (child actress)
Projects to carry out	Plan, organise and video a talent show / stage show / cabaret
Books to read	*101 Drama Games and Activities* by David Farmer (Lulu.com, 2007) *Amazing Grace* by Mary Hoffman (Frances Lincoln Children's Books, 1993) Resource: *Beginning Drama 4–11 (Early Years & Primary)* by Joe Winston and Miles Tandy (David Fulton Publishing, 2001)
Websites to visit	http://www.entsweb.co.uk/entertainers/index.html (directory of entertainers) http://www.rada.org/ (Royal Academy of Dramatic Art) http://www.spotlight.com/ (casting directory)
Places to go	National Media Museum, Bradford National Theatre, London Traverse Theatre, Edinburgh

     Permission to Photocopy

Historian

Excels in the understanding and investigation of historical events and in identifying patterns of events over time

Additional curriculum opportunities	Work with practising historians/archivists Study a favoured period of history in great detail Visit historical sites Examine historical artefacts and sources not normally available (e.g. special collections)
Learning materials	Artefacts Maps Photos Behind-the-scenes library access
People to study and aspire to	Michael Wood (historian and TV presenter) David Starkey (historian and TV presenter) Anna Keay (English Heritage's director of properties)
Projects to carry out	Assemble evidence and artefacts to prove a fictitious historical event, then make a convincing presentation
Books to read	*A History of Modern Britain* by Andrew Marr (Macmillan, 2007) *The Story of London: From Roman River to Capital City* by Jacqui Bailey and Christopher Maynard (A. & C. Black, 2000) *Timelines of World History* by John Teeple (Dorling Kindersley, 2006) *What If? Two: More Alternative Historical Time Lines* by Robert Blumetti (iUniverse, 2005) *Britannia: 100 Great Stories from British History* by Geraldine McCaughrean (Orion, 2004)
Websites to visit	http://www.bbc.co.uk/history (thorough and detailed historical information) http://www.english-heritage.org.uk (resources and places to visit) http://www.history.ac.uk (Institute of Historical Research)
Places to go	National Trust properties Ironbridge Gorge Museum, Telford Preston Hall Museum and Park, Stockton-on-Tees (includes a part-working Victorian street) Stonehenge, Avebury and other standing-stones sites

Musician

Excels in the composition, performance and appreciation of music

Additional curriculum opportunities	Enter music competitions Work with practising musicians Perform in front of a variety of audiences (sizes and ages) Compose and conduct others
Learning materials	Access to classical and popular music MP3 download sites Music software (e.g. Ableton, e-jay series) Variety of instruments Time to explore sounds, compose and perform
People to study and aspire to	Peter Gabriel (founder member of Genesis and champion of world music) Ben Mills (*X Factor* finalist) Nicola Benedetti (2004 BBC Young Musician of the Year)
Projects to carry out	Compose, rehearse and perform own piece entitled *Twenty-first Century Sound Garden*
Books to read	*Music Theory for Dummies* by Holly Day and Michael Pilhofer (Wiley, 2007) *Electronic and Experimental Music* by Thomas Holmes (Routledge, 2003) *The Classic FM Pocket Book of Music* by Darren Henley and Tim Lihoreau (Boosey and Hawkes, 2003)
Websites to visit	http://www.voicetraining.co.uk (Voice Gym – combining singing and Brain Gym) http://www.musicpreserved.org.uk (safeguarding our musical heritage) http://www.oddmusic.com/gallery (view and hear strange musical instruments)
Places to go	Charles Moore Collection of Musical Instruments, University of Leicester Mechanical Music Museum and Bygones, Cotton, Suffolk Liverpool Music Heritage: MP3 Audio Tour (http://www.liverpool08.com/)

    Permission to Photocopy

Storyteller

Excels in the verbal telling of stories from imagination and of real events (witnessed or second-hand)

Additional curriculum opportunities	Enter storytelling competitions Have time to develop and tell stories to a range of audiences Work with practising storytellers Listen to a variety of stories
Learning materials	DVD: Jim Henson's *The Storyteller* DVD: Jackanory – *Muddle Earth and the Magician of Samarkand* Digital audio recorder to rehearse and evaluate storytelling Webspace to upload own stories
People to study and aspire to	Christopher Kay (broadcaster and narrator of numerous audio books) Patrick Stewart (actor and teller of Dickens's tales on stage) Sue Perkins (winner of the World's Biggest Liar competition)
Projects to carry out	Research the world's greatest short story and retell it to an audience Hold your own World's Biggest Liar competition Arrange a storytelling competition in school
Books to read	*Tuesday* by David Weisner (Houghton Mifflin, 1998) – a wordless, richly illustrated fantasy for which learners invent their own story *Flotsam* by David Weisner (Clarion Books, 2006) – as above Resource: *The Magic of Metaphor: 77 Stories for Teachers, Trainers & Thinkers* by Nick Owen (Crown House, 2001)
Websites to visit	http://storynory.com/ (audio stories to download) http://www.scottishstorytellingcentre.co.uk (events, festival, CPD and much more) http://www.timsheppard.co.uk/story/tellinglinks.html (one of the web's largest storytelling resources)
Places to go	Museum of Myth and Fable, Wem, Shropshire Literary Festival, Hay-on-Wye, every May

Inventor

Excels in designing and successfully making original and interesting machines as solutions to problems

Additional curriculum opportunities	Work with practising inventors Have time, materials and tools to design and build own inventions Receive formative assessment on inventions Enter design/innovation competitions
Learning materials	Software: Crazy Machines (Viva Media) Gears, motors, pulleys, electrical control circuits, etc. Lego Mindstorms NXT®
People to study and aspire to	Cynthia Breazeal (internationally renowned robot designer) Eric Laithwaite (maverick scientist and inventor) László József Bíró (invented the ball-point pen)
Projects to carry out	Invent a teaching and learning machine Find out the world's biggest problem and invent a machine to solve it
Books to read	*1000 Inventions and Discoveries* by Roger Bridgman (Wiley, 2006) *How Things Work: The Physics of Everyday Life* by Louis Bloomfield (Wiley, 2005) *Inventing the Future: The Scientists who Changed our World* by John and Mary Gribbin (Puffin, 2004)
Websites to visit	http://www.makingthemodernworld.org.uk/ (inventions in daily life) http://www.bkfk.com/inventors/inventors.asp (famous inventors) http://www.grand-illusions.com/ (toys and ideas for enquiring minds)
Places to go	Intech Science Centre, Winchester The Lilliput Antique Doll and Toy Museum, Brading, Isle of Wight Making It! Discovery Centre, Mansfield, Nottinghamshire

Geographer

Excels in understanding the places, features and peoples of the world

Additional curriculum opportunities	Visit and study a variety of places – urban, suburban and country Work with practising geographers, geologists and earth scientists Have time and resources to study favourite places and peoples Prepare and carry out surveys of human behaviour
Learning materials	Maps Satellite navigation system Geographical atlases http://earth.google.com Digital camera and digital audio recorder
People to study and aspire to	Rita Gardner (director of the Royal Geographical Society) Nicholas Crane (geographer, journalist and TV presenter) Hermione Cockburn (TV presenter and earth scientist)
Projects to carry out	Prepare a geographical survey of a local nature reserve / village / estate Prepare cases in defence of and against a new building project
Books to read	*Wide Angle: National Geographic Greatest Places* by Ferdinand Protzman (National Geographic Books, 2005) *Earth from Above* by Yann Arthus-Bertrand (HNA Books, 2005) *Children Just Like Me* by Anabel Kindersley and Barnabas Kindersley (Dorling Kindersley, 1995)
Websites to visit	http://www.geographypages.co.uk (site of teachers' resources) http://www.globaldimension.org.uk (the world in your classroom) http://www.geographical.co.uk (UK geography magazine)
Places to go	Royal Geographical Society, London Bekonscot model village, Beaconsfield (or any model village) Sedgwick Museum of Earth Sciences, Cambridge

Linguist

Excels in understanding and using one or more languages – whether written, spoken or signed

Additional curriculum opportunities	Learn one or more languages in addition to first language Work with practising linguists/translators Speak and write languages with others fluent in them Visit places where languages other than first language are spoken
Learning materials	Translation dictionaries Phrase books DVD/CD language courses Films and media in languages other than first language
People to study and aspire to	Jacob Grimm (collector of fairy tales and co-founder of modern linguistics) J.R.R. Tolkien (author and professor of philology – love of words) Jean Aitchison (professor of language and communication)
Projects to carry out	Invent own alphabet / language / symbol system for communication
Books to read	*The Unfolding of Language* by Guy Deutscher (Arrow Books, 2006) *Dictionary of Languages: The Definitive Reference to more than 400 Languages* by Andrew Dalby (A.& C. Black, 2006) *The Languages of the World* by Kenneth Katzner (Routledge, 2002) *The Alphabet* by David Sacks (Hutchinson, 2003) *Linguistics: A Very Short Introduction* by P.H. Matthews (Oxford University Press, 2003)
Websites to visit	http://www.britishsignlanguage.com/ (themed visual BSL dictionary) http://www.google.com/language_tools (Google's free translation tool) http://www.ethnologue.com/ (catalogue of the world's 6912 known languages)
Places to go	A language museum for London was mooted in May 2007 by linguist David Crystal – hopefully to coincide with the 2012 Olympic Games Amgueddfa Genedlaethol Caerdydd (National Museum, Cardiff) British Library, London

Sports person

Excels in the strategic understanding and performance of one or more sports

Additional curriculum opportunities	Enter competitions and play competitively at local and national levels Train with professional sports people Have coaching and the time to dedicate to practice Study advanced aspects of technique and game play
Learning materials	Video to record and improve performance/technique Equipment of a standard matching level of play Footage of world champions to study
People to study and aspire to	Paula Radcliffe (world champion athlete) Tim Henman (dedicated and resilient tennis player) Dame Tanni Grey-Thompson (paralympic champion wheelchair athlete)
Projects to carry out	Prepare a coaching programme in chosen sport for a younger learner
Books to read	*Olympics* by Chris Oxlade and David Ballheimer (Dorling Kindersley, 2005) *The Race for the 2012 Olympics* by Mike Lee (Virgin Books, 2006) *Pitch Invasion: Adidas, Puma and the Making of Modern Sport* by Barbara Smit (Penguin, 2007) Resource: *Athletics Challenges: Aimed at KS3, KS4 and A Level* by Kevin Morgan (UWIC Press, 2001)
Websites to visit	http://www.olympic.org/uk/index_uk.asp (official Olympic Games website) http://www.ourkidsports.com/ (database of children's sport in the UK) http://news.bbc.co.uk/sport1/hi/academy/default.stm (useful information on over 20 popular sports)
Places to go	National Football Museum, Preston Warwickshire County Cricket Club Museum, Edgbaston Wimbledon Lawn Tennis Museum and Tour, London

Technologist

Excels in the understanding and use of technology, especially computers

Additional curriculum opportunities	Work with software designers / electronics engineers / communications engineers Explore the inner workings of older ICT equipment (unplugged and safe) Have the time to develop skills and understanding of technology Have the opportunity to assist a computer network manager in their role
Learning materials	Computer and appropriate software Safe, monitored access to technology discussion groups Internet access Range of digital equipment and media
People to study and aspire to	Bill Gates (entrepreneur, philanthropist and co-founder of Microsoft) Tim Berners-Lee (inventor of the world wide web) Steve Wozniak (co-founder of Apple and inventor of the original Apple 1 and 2 computers)
Projects to carry out	Design and build own computer Set up and manage own website Establish and grow an on-line community (with safety guidance)
Books to read	*The New How Things Work: From Lawn Mowers to Surgical Robots and Everything in between* by John Langone (National Geographic, 2004) *Star Wars: the New Essential Guide to Weapons and Technology* by W. Haden Blackman (Del Rey Books, 2004) *Second Lives* by Tim Guest (Hutchinson, 2007) – all about on-line communities
Websites to visit	http://www.focusmag.co.uk/ (BBC's Science and Technology magazine on-line) http://www.21stcentury.co.uk/ (information about the latest technological discoveries and gadgets) http://www.computersciencelab.com/ComputerHistory/History.htm (visual history of computing)
Places to go	Museum of Computing, University of Bath in Swindon Computer Museum at Bletchley Park, Milton Keynes Apple Store, Regent's Street, London

Author

Excels in the writing of stories, poems, reports and other forms of text

Additional curriculum opportunities	Enter writing and poetry competitions Work with practising authors Visit a publisher's offices and print works Have time for extended writing and to receive formative assessment on work
Learning materials	Word processor Dictionaries and thesauri
People to study and aspire to	Philip Pullman (children's writer – *Northern Lights*, 1995) David Almond (children's writer – *Skellig*, 1998) Diana Wynne Jones (children's writer – *Howl's Moving Castle*, 1988)
Projects to carry out	Write, edit, illustrate, design and produce own book of short stories / poems Organise the production of the above
Books to read	*The 38 Most Common Fiction Writing Mistakes* by Jack M. Bickham (Writer's Digest Books, 1998) *The Children's Writers' and Artists' Yearbook 2008* (A. & C. Black, 2007) *What If?: Writing Exercises for Fiction Writers* by Anne Bernays and Pamela Painter (HarperCollins, 1991)
Websites to visit	http://www.literacytrust.org.uk/ (building a literate nation) http://www.bridportprize.org.uk/juniorindex.htm (poetry and short story competition) http://www.bbc.co.uk/worldservice/arts/features/howtowrite/index.shtml (straightforward writing advice)
Places to go	Writers' Museum, Edinburgh Poetry Library at the South Bank Centre, London Dublin Writers Museum, Dublin

Leader

Excels in the organisation, motivation and management of other people to complete tasks

Additional curriculum opportunities	Lead a variety of teams/groups Work with older, more experienced leaders Watch recordings of world leaders in action Receive feedback from the group/team on own leadership skills Have time to reflect on own style of leadership
Learning materials	Checklist of leadership actions (communicate, set a goal, involve everyone, don't boss, etc.)
People to study and aspire to	Victoria Hale (social entrepreneur bringing medicine to the developing world) Kofi Annan (ex-Secretary General of the United Nations and Nobel Peace Prize recipient) Karren Brady (MD of Birmingham City Football Club, a director of Mothercare and Channel 4 TV)
Projects to carry out	From scratch: build, organise and motivate a team to solve a school problem (e.g. reviving an unused area or updating an outdated one)
Books to read	*Mohandas Gandhi* (Pull Ahead Biographies) by Sheila Rivera (Lerner Publications, 2007) *On Leadership: Practical Wisdom from the People who Know* by Allan Leighton (Random House, 2007) *Project Management Skills for Kids* by Robert Cassella (Trafford, 2003)
Websites to visit	http://www.careeracademies.org.uk (looking to the future for our next generation of business leaders) http://www.leadership-tools.com/leadership-skills-for-kids.html (a description of children's leadership skills) http://gardenofpraise.com (biographies of famous world leaders)
Places to go	Le Mémorial de Caen, France (especially the Nobel Prize winners gallery) Houses of Parliament, London Scottish Parliament in Holyrood Park, Edinburgh

   Permission to Photocopy

Mechanic

Excels in the ability to understand, (dis)assemble and fix machines

Additional curriculum opportunities	Investigate and learn by touching and manipulating Work with practising mechanics and mechanical engineers Have time to investigate and fix machines Visit engineering works and workshops Work and learn with site manager
Learning materials	Crazy Machines: The Wacky Contraptions Games (Viva Media) Variety of tools and equipment Engineering diagrams Haynes manuals
People to study and aspire to	Steve Matchett (Top Formula One pit crew mechanic) Abigail Sprankling (REME captain and Engineer of the Year, 2005) Katy Deacon (IET Young Woman Engineer of the Year, 2006)
Projects to carry out	Create a visual/audio/written troubleshooting guide for a car/computer/toaster or other machine
Books to read	*The New Way Things Work* by David Macaulay (Dorling Kindersley, 1998) *How our Car Works* by Larry Burkett and Ed Strauss (Faith Kidz, 2002) *Sneaky Uses for Everyday Things* by Cy Tymony (Andrews McMeel, 2003)
Websites to visit	http://www.howstuffworks.com (wide-ranging descriptions of machines and artefacts) http://www.familycar.com/Classroom (how cars work) http://www.engc.org.uk/ (UK Engineering Council) http://www.imagineeringweb.co.uk (stimulating interest in engineering) http://www.youngeng.org/home.asp (inspiring our young engineers)
Places to go	British Lawnmower Museum, Southport Goodwood Festival of Speed, Chichester REME Museum of Technology, Arborfield, Berkshire

Comedian

Excels at making others laugh, cheering them up, and seeing the positive/funny side of difficult situations

Additional curriculum opportunities	Recount funny stories and tell jokes to a variety of audiences Measure impact of own humour Work with practising comedians Watch comedians performing on DVD Put forward 'the funny side' when studying aspects of curriculum subjects
Learning materials	Props Microphone Stool Smoke-filled bar (minus smoke and alcohol)
People to study and aspire to	Bill Bailey (nearly clean, clever, multi-talented comedian) Rowan Atkinson (pioneering comedy actor and writer) Laurel and Hardy (masters of visual comedy)
Projects to carry out	Write, rehearse and perform own stand-up comedy routine
Books to read	*Getting the Joke: The Art of Stand-up Comedy* by Oliver Double (Methuen Drama, 2005) *The Rough Guide to British Cult Comedy* by Julian Hall (Rough Guides, 2006) *The Naked Jape: Uncovering the Hidden World of Jokes* by Jimmy Carr and Lucy Greeves (Michael Joseph, 2007)
Websites to visit	http://www.jamescampbell.info/ (James Campbell – popular children's stand-up comedian) http://www.kidsjokes.co.uk/ (jokes for kids) http://www.thecomedystore.co.uk/ (centre of the comedy universe)
Places to go	Gnome Magic, Colchester Edinburgh Fringe Festival

All-round Learner

Excels in ability to learn across a broad range of subjects and skills

Additional curriculum opportunities	Study the learning process and parts of the brain
	Discover own preferred learning style – developing strengths, building on weaknesses
	Access an extended curriculum covering more subjects and different methods of learning (e.g. Chinese, horse-riding, geology)
	Study the methods and personal qualities of more experienced learners
	Have time to follow own areas of interest
Learning materials	Library
	Internet
	Experts
	ICT equipment
	Traditional materials (pen and notebook, etc.)
People to study and aspire to	Sir Jonathan Miller (neurologist, theatre and opera director, television presenter, humorist and sculptor)
	Bill Lucas (champion of the Learning to Learn movement)
	Despina Panayi (Outstanding New Teacher of the Year, 2007, London)
Projects to carry out	A self-chosen, self-directed investigation and presentation into any subject that is not on the curriculum
Books to read	Any!
Websites to visit	http://www.sciencemuseum.org.uk/on-line/brain/index.asp (clear, uncluttered information about the brain)
	http://www.bbc.co.uk/learning/ (good starting point for a learning journey)
	http://www.bl.uk/ (British Library – the world's knowledge)
Places to go	British Schools Museum, Hitchin, Hertfordshire
	Look Out Discovery Centre, Bracknell, Berkshire
	Museum of Childhood, Edinburgh

Problem-solver

Excels in the ability to find practical and effective solutions to a range of problems (not just in mathematics)

Additional curriculum opportunities	Offer solutions to a wide range of problems: subject-based and practical (around the school / in the classroom) Learn about different problem-solving strategies Study more experienced problem-solvers to establish what they do and how they do it View the content of different subject areas as problems to be solved rather than knowledge to be gained
Learning materials	Problem-solving processes and checklists
People to study and aspire to	John de Chastelain (retired soldier and diplomat who helped solve Northern Ireland's decommissioning problem) Albert Einstein ('It's not that I'm so smart, it's just that I stay with problems longer') Carol Vorderman (TV personality and mathematical problem-solver)
Projects to carry out	Create a flow-chart for solving any problem Select a problem from the world's news and think up several solutions
Books to read	*Thinkertoys: A Handbook of Creative-Thinking Techniques* by Michael Michalko (Ten Speed Press, 2006) *How to Have Kick-Ass Ideas* by Chris Barez-Brown (Harper Element, 2006) *The Thinker's Toolkit: 14 Powerful Techniques for Problem Solving* by Morgan Jones (Three Rivers Press, 1998)
Websites to visit	http://www.ericdigests.org/pre-9213/cooperative.htm (starting points for co-operative problem-solving in the classroom) http://www.mindtools.com/pages/main/newMN_TMC.htm (guidance for solving problems) http://en.wikipedia.org/wiki/Seven_Bridges_of_K%C3%B6nigsberg (intriguing real-life problem) http://www.jimloy.com/puzz/puzz.htm (puzzle central)
Places to go	Inspire Discovery Centre, Norwich Robolab and Mindstorms (part of Legoland, Windsor) Design Museum, London

Team Player

Excels in the ability to work collaboratively in a team/group, to understand the needs of others and to form enduring social relationships/friendships

Additional curriculum opportunities	Contribute in a variety of teams and groups Reflect on own collaborative skills Work and learn in groups with older and/or more effective members Meet a wide range of people and work with them
Learning materials	Classroom organisation to support collaboration
People to study and aspire to	Raymond Meredith Belbin (groundbreaking research into team roles) Matt Lucas (half of the Little Britain team) James Cracknell (member of Britain's Olympic gold-medal-winning rowing four)
Projects to carry out	Select a problem – school/local/national/global – and then suggest a 'dream team' of people who could work together to solve it
Books to read	*Team Building through Physical Challenges* by Donald R. Glover and Daniel W. Midura (Human Kinetics Europe, 1992) *Team-building Activities for Every Group* by Alanna Jones (Rec Room, 1999) Resource: *Collaborative Learning Techniques: A Practical Guide to Promoting Learning in Groups* by Thomas A. Angelo et al. (Jossey Bass Wiley, 2004)
Websites to visit	http://tlt.its.psu.edu/suggestions/teams/index.html (What are teams? How do they work?) http://www.queendom.com/tests/access_page (free and detailed emotional intelligence test) http://www.workingwithothers.org (teamwork to improve schools, from University of Brighton) http://www.discovery-project.com (emotional intelligence in schools and the community)
Places to go	Open Door Adventure, Denbighshire, North Wales Robogeddon, Somerset (teams designing robots) Challenger Learning Centre, National Space Centre, Leicester Camp Beaumont, Norfolk, Wolverhampton and the Isle of Wight

Mystic

Excels in the understanding of religious and/or spiritual concepts

Additional curriculum opportunities	Have time to reflect on experiences and ideas Work with spiritual/religious leaders Meditate/pray Meet people from a wide range of religious traditions Hear myths and stories from around the world
Learning materials	Shap Pictorial Calendar of Religious Festivals Space and time A quiet area
People to study and aspire to	Deepak Chopra (author and world-renowned spiritual guide) Joseph Campbell (author and researcher into the world of myths and legends) Anthony de Mello (writer and spiritual guide)
Projects to carry out	Write, set to music and record/perform a relaxation meditation
Books to read	*World Religions* by John Bowker (Dorling Kindersley, 1997) Resources: *Children and Spirituality* – an excellent leaflet from the Mothers' Union (http://www.themothersunion.org/resources_for_children.aspx) *Baby Buddhas: A Guide for Teaching Meditation to Children* by Lisa Desmond (Andrews McMeel, 2004)
Websites to visit	http://www.worldreligions.co.uk (photos from the world's major religions) http://www.shap.org/ (supporting the study and teaching of world religions) http://www.learningmeditation.com/children.htm (audio meditation resources for use with children) http://www.worldprayers.org (great prayers for across all religious traditions)
Places to go	World Peace Buddhist Temple, Ulverston, Cumbria Bede's World, Jarrow, Tyne and Wear Places of worship for major religions

     Permission to Photocopy

Philosopher

Excels in the ability to contemplate life, the universe and everything by asking deep questions and seeking a range of answers

Additional curriculum opportunities	Ask challenging questions and receive supportive responses Work with practising philosophers Have time to think Be challenged by intellectual equals
Learning materials	Mind Space Time
People to study and aspire to	Rene Descartes ('I think, therefore I am') Friedrich Nietzsche (one of the fathers of existentialism) Dame Mary Warnock (British philosopher, social and ethical thinker)
Projects to carry out	Set up and run a debate on a hot topic (war / global warming, etc.)
Books to read	*Philosophy: A Very Short Introduction* by Edward Craig (Oxford Paperbacks, 2002) *Ethics: A Very Short Introduction* by Simon Blackburn (Oxford Paperbacks, 2003) Resources: *But Why? Developing Philosophical Thinking in the Classroom* by Sara Stanley and Steve Bowkett (NEP, 2004) Newswise – subscription-based resource to stimulate the thoughtful debate of topical issues (http://www.dialogueworks.co.uk/newswise/index.html)
Websites to visit	http://www.ashidakim.com/zenkoans/zenindex.html (Buddhist conundrums to get minds in a tangle) http://sapere.org.uk/what-is-p4c/ (about philosophy for children) http://www.familiesonline.co.uk/article/static/248 (about big questions from little minds) http://royalinstitutephilosophy.org/think/articles.php (articles from *Think* magazine) http://users.ox.ac.uk/~worc0337/phil_topics.html (everything you ever wanted to know about philosophy)
Places to go	Red House, Bexleyheath, home of William Morris, artist and philosopher Public lectures on philosophical topics

Risk-taker

Excels in the ability to make informed judgements, then have the confidence to take planned and calculated risks

Additional curriculum opportunities	Take emotional, physical and intellectual risks (within safe, legal, agreed limits) Set a learning goal that appears unachievable, then go for it Study people who have taken risks and succeeded/failed Distinguish 'reckless' from 'calculated'
Learning materials	Opportunity
People to study and aspire to	Sir Ranulph Fiennes (polar explorer) Jacques Cousteau (underwater explorer) Natasza Zurek (world-class snowboarder)
Projects to carry out	Identify the world's top ten risk-takers and top ten risks Assist in the risk assessment of a school visit
Books to read	*The Man who Walked between the Towers* by Mordicai Gerstein (Roaring Brook Press, 2003) *SAS Survival Guide: How to Survive Anywhere, on Land or at Sea* by John Wiseman (Collins Gem, 2004) *Outside the Box 9–11* by Molly Potter (A. & C. Black, 2007)
Websites to visit	http://www.pamf.org/teen/life/risktaking/#Healthy%20Risks (healthy vs unhealthy risks) http://www.creativity-portal.com/bc/taking.risks.html (short piece on creativity and risk-taking)
Places to go	The Adventure Rope Course, Shropshire and Tunbridge Wells NCCL Galleries of Justice, Nottingham

In England, the extended schools agenda paves the way for greater parental involvement and broader community links with schools. Regardless of national initiatives, this outward-looking approach offers wonderful opportunities for enriching your GAT provision.

Parents, guardians and long-term carers, after all, are the true experts when the specialist subject is their children. They often supply realistic and useful information that helps in the assessment of giftedness and talent. They also offer a rich and varied source of experience and knowledge. On the other hand, once their child has been identified as GAT, they may need support and information regarding provision and entitlement in school.

In 1992, B. Lewis and M. Louis found that parents were correct 61 per cent of the time when identifying giftedness in their children. The remaining 39 per cent were right in saying that their child was above average, but the child didn't meet certain GAT criteria. ('Parental Beliefs about Giftedness in Young Children and their Relation to Actual Ability Level', *Gifted Children Quarterly*, No. 36, 27–31). Whether parents overestimate or underestimate abilities, let them describe their child to you in positive terms.

The local community is full of people and organisations whose daily work will prove fascinating to GAT learners with a specific expertise: gifted scientists will benefit from links with the local chemical plant, talented leaders can aspire to the lives of businessmen and women, and local colleges and training organisations provide opportunities to see and experience the next level of education.

Building relationships with parents

With GAT learners in mind, take time to reach out to parents and the community. Good relationships with parents have three main features:

- Inform:
  - ❑ anticipate the information that parents need and provide it in a user-friendly style before you are asked for it;
  - ❑ respond quickly and accurately to requests for additional information.
- Involve:
  - ❑ provide opportunities for parents to take part in all aspects of school life;
  - ❑ discover, value and use parents' skills and talents in school.
- Interact:
  - ❑ show an interest in parents and their lives;
  - ❑ ask questions, respond to their replies, share a little of yourself;
  - ❑ respect them and appreciate the joint responsibility that you both hold for their children;
  - ❑ be proactive – take the initiative in person or by phone, email or letter.

These three elements weave together into an ethos and an approach to parent contact. The strength of the relationships which follow will determine the quality of support you receive from home and the ease with which problems and challenges can be resolved. Your investment will be paid back.

Talk to them

Your relationship with a GAT learner's parents, guardians or carers will contribute to your understanding of their child's particular strengths and learning needs. In reality there is limited time for this – often only a termly parents' evening and a word at the school gate now and then. It's important therefore to make effective use of these meetings.

Whenever you are with a parent, build the relationship, ask the right questions, listen carefully to replies and keep the following in mind:

1. Does this parent believe that their child is gifted, able and/or talented?
2. What is this parent telling me about their child's strengths and interests?
3. Is this parent gifted, able and talented? If so, in what areas?

A direct 'Do you think your child is gifted/able/talented?' is not recommended as a starting point unless parents have a clear understanding of exactly what you mean. At formal parents' evenings, you may wish to ask and note down:

1. What does your child do best?
2. What is your child most interested in?
3. How does your child spend their free time?
4. Where do your child's talents lie?

Tell them

I recommend shrewd management and careful thought when presenting information to parents. This information can be divisive and may fracture the support that you already have from the wider parent community. To help you think this through, compare and contrast these two scenarios.

Scenario 1: Send a letter to the parents of all GAT learners informing them of their child's learning strengths and inviting them to an after-school meeting. At this meeting, explain national, local and school thinking around GAT provision and describe how you identify and support these children. Describe (or demonstrate) how this is put into practice. Invite these parents into school to share their own gifts and talents, and then provide details of resources (books/clubs/websites/events/organisations) to support the GAT learners out of school. Suggest and model ways in which parents can extend and enrich their GAT child's learning at home.

Scenario 2: Send a letter to all parents inviting them to a meeting about the school's approach to teaching and learning. Include in this an explanation of national, local and school thinking around GAT provision and describe how you identify and support these children. Describe (or demonstrate) how this is put into practice. Explain that whether a child is identified as GAT or not, the school endeavours to provide appropriate experiences. Invite the parents into school to share their own gifts and talents and then provide details of resources (books/clubs/websites/

events/organisations) to support the out-of-school learning of all children. Suggest and model ways in which parents can extend and enrich their child's learning at home.

I'd advise you to take the second approach because of its inclusivity. GAT is incorporated as an important part of teaching and learning. The first approach is élitist and divisive (unless you've identified everyone in the school as GAT). Scenario 2 offers all parents information and support, regardless of their child's specific strengths and needs. And if they are clear up front about the origin of 'GAT status', then there is a basis for positive discussion later on.

Handle them effectively

Even with the most careful planning and presentation of your GAT approach, it's best to be prepared for challenges. Here are some 'interesting' parents that you may wish to plan for:

- Insists that their child is GAT when they clearly are not.
- Insists that their child is not GAT when clearly they are.
- Has correctly identified their child as GAT and has the time, skills and resources to work with you to extend them.
- Feels unable to support their child at the level they need.

- Is pushing their GAT child too far too soon.
- Is using GAT status as an excuse for misbehaviour and attendance issues.
- Wants help managing behaviour at home.
- Is jealous of the GAT status of other children.
- Wants to home educate.

At your next GAT staff meeting, have some fun role-playing the situations. Make sure you take away a valuable learning experience. Clarify and agree whole-school responses and strategies for managing these and similar situations. That parent could be waiting for you at the classroom door tomorrow.

Using parents' interests, work and careers: I propose that all parents have something to offer GAT learners (whether they realise it or not). Your expectations of them will contribute to their own self-belief and willingness to get involved with school life. See the potential in each parent to contribute their skills, experience and knowledge to your teaching and the children's learning. Be interested in their lives and work and make it clear that your door is open (check school policy on inviting adult visitors in first). However, do be sensitive: some parents may be anxious about working in school and may not fully understand why you value their skills.

Parent's skills	*Suggested involvement with GAT learners*
Taxi driving (full-time – work)	Taxi drivers often develop phenomenal visual memories. Use this skill to show learners how visual thinking, memory and imagination can work. Link to map work and topics on the local and wider communities.

Parent's skills	Suggested involvement with GAT learners
Nursing (intensive care – work)	Intensive care nurses require enormous emotional and practical strength. Use their experience to show learners how emotional intelligence develops and is used. Link to work in PSHE and science.
Playing an instrument (guitar in local band – hobby)	Musicians derive a great deal of satisfaction from playing alone and together. Use their experience to show learners the results of practising and the benefits of collaborating. Link to work in music and drama.
Motherhood (full-time – not a hobby)	Mothers carry great responsibility and call on a range of social, emotional and practical skills. Use their experience to show learners what life-organisation is like. Link to work in PSHE.
Artist (full-time for local authority – work)	Artists express the world in creative and intriguing ways. Use their experience to inspire learners to create their own art and extend their understanding of art and artists. Link to work in art and DT.
Building (unskilled manual labour – work)	Builders rely on physical strength, agility, and practical and visual intelligence. Use their experience to show learners how things are constructed and to enhance their skills. Link to work in DT, maths.
Writing (published poetry – hobby)	Poets use language simply and effectively to describe things. Use their experience to inspire learners to create their own poems and to extend their understanding of poetry. Link to work in literacy.

Supporting parents: Sir Christopher Ball, linguist and champion of twenty-first century learning, serves the world of education in many valuable ways, not least through the practicality of his thinking and the clarity of his communication. His 'Conditions for High Achievement' provide us with a deceptively simple plan for nurturing gifts, talents and abilities. Conditions for high achievement:

- Warm, demanding adults
- Exploratory, negotiated informal learning opportunities
- Access to people outside peer group
- One outrageous learning success.

These conditions must appear in school and at home. Here are some ideas for helping parents to achieve them in the midst of hectic family lives.

What it means: Loving but not soft, challenging but not severe, supportive but not overprotective – a tricky balance to keep, but achievable. Parents need to love, appreciate and encourage their children and at the same time have high expectations of them. High expectations without warmth may lead to stress; warmth without high expectations may lead to apathy and overreliance.

How to support parents: Suggest that they simultaneously express both warmth and high expectation:

- 'Wow [smiles] – your drawing has really improved [ruffles child's hair] – now, what about painting?'
- '10 out of 10 in maths [punches air] – fantastic [hugs child] – I think we need some harder questions next time.'

As a resource to assist, offer the following words to stick on the fridge/kitchen door. Be sure to advise parents to omit the expectation now and again. Children may be left feeling that their achievements are never good enough if they always hear 'That's brilliant, *but* …' or 'That's super *and* …'.

Praise bank: Well done, fantastic, wow, super, great work, wonderful, excellent, nice one, beautiful, incredible, outstanding, brilliant, dazzling, first rate, superb, tremendous, stunning, eye-catching, amazing, magnificent, splendid, glorious, clever, smart

Expectation bank: I expect, I'm looking forward to, I hope, What's next?, I wonder if …, I know you can, I believe that you will …, Soon you will …, Where to next?, How can we make it even better?, Imagine …, Just suppose …, Looking ahead …, Eventually, Sooner or later

Exploratory, negotiated informal learning opportunities

What it means: Learning which is child led, open ended and supported by involved adults. Parents give their children confidence and opportunities to choose learning resources and experiences. Parents need to provide 'structured, supported freedom' – learning with wide boundaries.

How to support parents: To support GAT learners, parents should:

1. Know, accept and value their children's areas of ability.
2. Budget their time: allocate and ring fence quality time with children.
3. Understand that when learning, children like to explore and follow their own interests. (Tell parents more about learning, in person or through a leaflet. Call it 'How Children Learn'.)
4. Suggest to their children starting points for learning (linked to areas of ability), for example:
   - a) places to visit
   - b) books/magazines to read
   - c) people to talk to
   - d) clubs to join
   - e) websites to visit, on-line communities to join, web searches to make
   - f) questions to ask
   - g) TV programmes / films to watch
   - h) radio shows to listen to
   - i) things to make/buy
   - j) pod/web casts to listen to / view
   - k) campaigns to join.
5. Oversee their children's explorations and intervene when necessary.

Here's how this might work in practice

Molly's mum wants to support her 11-year-old daughter's talent on the saxophone, but works and has three other children to nurture and a husband who works away from home. In a rare 3.5 minutes' peace and quiet, she makes a mental plan after receiving a GAT suggestion sheet from Molly's school.

Molly's mum's plan

1. Molly has achieved Grade 5 on the saxophone. I think she's great and I enjoy hearing her practise.

2. I can give her 10 minutes tonight after the others have gone to bed, 10 minutes tomorrow and half an hour at the weekend, and maybe a few hours next week when my husband's back home.

3. Molly needs a push to get her started, but once she's interested in something I can't tear her away.

4. Starting points: I'm going to challenge Molly to go on-line, find a jazz concert taking place locally in the next few weeks and do a profile of the artist. If she succeeds we'll book tickets and go.

5. I got her started but she wasn't interested at first. The following day I tried again and she was away like a shot. At the weekend I read her profile of the artist and arranged for her dad to take her to the concert. She even booked tickets on-line. With my credit card. Dark times a'coming.

More access to others than peer group

What it means: By definition GAT learners achieve far more (in certain areas) than most others to whom they are compared. Safe access to a wide variety of interesting people is key to a rich life experience.

How to support parents: Show parents the value of exposing their children to a variety of people and advise them to maximise this – always bearing safety in mind. Here are some examples.

Access to ….	Potential benefit for child
Beaver/Brownie/ Guide/Scout leader	Seeing leadership in action; interaction with non-school/non-parent adult; developing sense of humour, interpersonal skills, discipline
Grandparent	Experiencing wisdom, time, acceptance, freedom, treats, history, love, stories, safe places to experiment (shed/garden/kitchen)
Swimming coach	Learn dedication, mental and physical endurance, persistence, stamina, competitive thinking
Museum or city tour guide	Learn interesting facts behind the scenes of a place, see how others present information to strangers, see what confidence looks like
Neighbour (folk singer or guitarist)	Learn about folk music and playing the guitar/singing, performing, memorising words, rhyming, socialising

One outrageous learning success (OLS)

What it means: As I write this my own dyslexic GAT daughter has just received her SATs results. She got straight 5s and achieved 100 per cent in two maths papers. She's had an outrageous success and whatever failures or further successes come her way, those 5s will give her security in her abilities and the confidence to achieve.

How to support parents: SATs results can provide an OLS – but for only a small number of children. Everyone deserves an OLS and parents can help provide the opportunities.

Vicky's and Luke's story

Vicky is 37 years old, a GAT mathematician, and is raising three young GAT boys (Luke, Jack and Dan). Her experience as a parent of GAT learners and her relationship with her sons' school provides us with a lot to think about as we plan our approach to working with parents.

At school Vicky excelled in maths but played it down because it was safer to stay 'under the radar'. Her teachers did not recognise her abilities. When her boys came along she passed this attitude on to them. She instinctively knew their various talents but made sure they hid them in school. She and her partner never made a big deal about their children's gifts.

Then one day it hit her: *If someone runs 100 m in under 10 seconds we get all excited, jump up and down and give them a medal. But if someone gets 100 per cent in a maths test they'd better keep their head down in case they're called a swot. If they celebrate it's like they're showing off. It's not right.*

I've constantly been telling Luke to dumb down. Yes, he's a natural at maths and literacy, but he does work hard as well. I make sure at home that he's got things to keep him occupied at his level. I'm really cross that he's never been mentioned in the school's praise assemblies. He always gets 100 per cent in his tests. He knows he's achieving but he's not recognised for it. I think there's something wrong if he always gets 100 per cent. The work's not challenging him.

Vicky told me that Luke's behaviour at home is erratic. Over the years she's noticed a pattern:

If Luke's getting work that he enjoys, and if it stretches him, then he's OK at home. If he's bored, then we have problems. He's generally OK at school. He just puts up with it.

Vicky's second child (Jack) is a gifted mathematician too, but she believes her third boy, Dan, is the most able. Of the three, Dan's the one who doesn't appear on the school's GAT register.

Dan can out-argue me. I have trouble winning when we debate things or get into an argument. His concept of language is amazing and he's an incredibly quick thinker. But unfortunately his gifts don't seem to tick any boxes at school. He doesn't fit neatly in the gifted box so his talents'll go unnoticed unless I make a fuss or unless his teacher looks a little bit deeper.

Visitors and visits

Parents offer a wide range of valuable experiences. Where there's a gap they can't fill, look to local organisations. Invite individuals or groups into school or go to them. There are several ways to do this:

- Organise after-school trips for GAT learners that match specialism to organisation (e.g. mathematics – building society; language – publisher; music – concert hall).

- Invite in groups that offer something to all children yet target GAT (e.g. an Indian dance troupe if your school has several GAT dancers, a theatre workshop if your school has several GAT actors).
- Ensure that trips appeal to GAT learners at their level.
- Make sure that trip leaders know who the GAT learners are and plan for them.
- Hold a talent day at which several visitors come in to share their expertise.
- Look out for local events especially for GAT learners (local authority GAT days; private GAT organisations or clubs with taster sessions).
- Ask your GAT learners whom they would like to meet and where they would like to go.

As always, check school policy on inviting adult visitors in.

Local, national and global

GAT learners may aspire to local, national and international participation and success, especially if their gifts, talents and abilities are deemed significant not only in school but further afield. I suggest three ways to involve your GAT learners in life outside the school community.

Communication

GAT learners sometimes feel isolated and alone, believing that no one shares their level of skill and world view. It may help to hook up these learners with others of a similar proficiency and disposition – their true peers. With successful contact, both parties may feel more confident about who they are and may also take each other's expertise further. Use your own networks to find, contact and link to schools locally, nationally and worldwide who are willing to help.

Feel free to post requests or offer contact via the discussion boards on my website: www.thinkingclassroom.co.uk/ShowForums.aspx

Participation

GAT learners' achievements may outgrow the school. Liaise with parents and plan for this. If 9-year-old Dale is a Black Belt (Second Dan), don't limit him to the after-school Judo Club unless he's helping others with less expertise.

For every GAT specialism there are opportunities to take part in extended learning, events and competitions locally, nationally and even internationally. Always be on the look-out for activities and events that will appeal to and challenge your GAT learners.

Participation works both ways. A GAT learner has a lot to offer the wider community and may consider using and developing their skills by:

- teaching and coaching others
- running master classes
- contributing to specialist books, newspapers, magazines and websites
- helping others to get started
- working in local shops/organisations linked to their interests
- volunteering for related charity work
- campaigning
- setting up their own businesses.

Learners who've had a hard time of being talented in school may find meaning and purpose outside it.

Extension

Universities and colleges often provide opportunities for GAT learners. Just look at the potential benefits to a young and gifted mathematician of attending an astrophysics lecture at university:

- place to aim for (university course)
- understanding of how university works
- feeling special and honoured to be out of school
- high-level knowledge to assimilate
- experts to quiz
- students to admire and aspire to
- experience of higher learning
- subject content and books to pore over.

Contact tertiary education institutions to find out if they offer resources and experiences to younger GAT learners. If not, try to arrange something anyway – maybe a trip behind the scenes or sitting in on a couple of lectures.

Leading the way in England is the National Academy for Gifted and Talented Youth (NAGTY) based at the University of Warwick: www.nagty.ac.uk

8. I need to conclude with a summary of this book

Over the preceding pages you've learned about the academic and emotional needs of GAT learners and addressed practical ways to include them in your everyday teaching and learning.

From the start I left the definition of GAT learners broad and deep – in that way I've kept the door wide open so that as many learners as possible can step through and be valued for what they do best. However, remember that there exist truly exceptional children who fall outside any categorisation – those whose abilities are so far developed that the standard school experience does not do them justice. In these cases at least you now have methods of identification and possible ways forward.

I hope you will be able to develop your role with GAT learners, whether as a class teacher, GAT co-ordinator, school leader, consultant or adviser. You've had the opportunity to build up your knowledge and skills in:

- identifying learners
- managing provision
- enriching thinking
- enriching emotional intelligence
- enriching the curriculum
- involving parents and the wider community.

Therefore you have developed key areas in your support of these pupils.

No single book can hope to cover all aspects of GAT policy and provision, and I'm sure you've developed many resources and techniques of your own that could have won a place in these pages. You, after all, are a creative professional. You're in the business of creating professional educational solutions for your learners.

It would be wonderful if this last part of the book were seen not as an end but a beginning. The pooled talents and experience of every person who reads this sentence would be phenomenal. If each of you shared just one of your GAT ideas, we'd have a superb open and free resource. To facilitate this, I've created an area of my website for GAT resources and discussion. You'll find versions of the expert support packs (see Chapter 6) there to add to and opportunities to discuss GAT-related issues.

Go visit www.thinkingclassroom.co.uk/GAT

9. Resources

Here is a small selection of websites to support your GAT work:

www.brookes.ac.uk/schools/education/rescon/cpdgifted

Oxford Brookes' Westminster Institute of Education

Resources and advice for professionals such as GAT co-ordinators, teachers, governors, teacher trainers. Includes a good selection of lesson plans for history, maths, music and science.

www.standards.dcsf.gov.uk/giftedandtalented

The standards site of the Department for Children, Schools and Families

Provides government policy and advice for identifying GAT learners and providing for them.

www.nagty.ac.uk

National Academy for Gifted and Talented Youth

Set up by the government in 2002 to improve GAT teaching and learning. Includes research, CPD materials and useful free downloads, including back issues of *G&T Update*.

www.nace.co.uk

National Association for Able Children in Education

An independent organisation for educators working with GAT learners. Offers high-quality conferences, CPD resources, and publications for all age groups.

www.nagcbritain.org.uk

National Association for Gifted Children

A charity offering advice and support for families of GAT learners and organisations involved with them. Information for schools and activities for three age groups – up to 5, 5–10 and 11–18.

www.ablepupils.com

Scottish Network for Able Pupils

Information for teachers, learners and parents on more able children.

www2.teachernet.gov.uk

Site offering comprehensive support for GAT educators. Includes resources, information on GAT, national quality standards and lots of straightforward advice and information.

www.ygt.dcsf.gov.uk

The government's centralised on-line resource for GAT standards and provision.